Ministry
Rediscovered

Text copyright © Mike Starkey 2011
The author asserts the moral right
to be identified as the author of this work

Published by
The Bible Reading Fellowship
15 The Chambers, Vineyard
Abingdon OX14 3FE
United Kingdom
Tel: +44 (0)1865 319700
Email: enquiries@brf.org.uk
Website: www.brf.org.uk
BRF is a Registered Charity

ISBN 978 1 84101 616 0

First published 2011
10 9 8 7 6 5 4 3 2 1 0
All rights reserved

Acknowledgments
Unless otherwise stated, scripture quotations are taken from the Holy Bible, New International Version, copyright © 1973, 1978, 1984 by International Bible Society, are used by permission of Hodder & Stoughton Publishers, a member of the Hachette Livre Group UK. All rights reserved. 'NIV' is a registered trademark of International Bible Society. UK trademark number 1448790.

Scripture quotations from The New Revised Standard Version of the Bible, Anglicised Edition, copyright © 1989, 1995 by the Division of Christian Education of the National Council of the Churches of Christ in the United States of America, are used by permission. All rights reserved.

Extracts from the Authorised Version of the Bible (The King James Bible), the rights in which are vested in the Crown, are reproduced by permission of the Crown's Patentee, Cambridge University Press.

Extract from 'Evening Prayer', *Lutheran Book of Worship*, © Augsburg Fortress. Used by kind permission of the publisher.

The paper used in the production of this publication was supplied by mills that source their raw materials from sustainably managed forests. Soy-based inks were used in its printing and the laminate film is biodegradable.

A catalogue record for this book is available from the British Library

Printed in Singapore by Craft Print International Ltd

Ministry
Rediscovered

Shaping a unique and creative church

Mike Starkey

Contents

1. A very personal journey 7

2. Cloning the church 23
   Snapshot: From the ashes 38

3. The call to creativity 40
   Snapshot: Urban arts 58

4. Unique church 60
   Snapshot: Cake on Wednesday 90

5. Unique leader 92
   Snapshot: The guitar club 105

6. Rethinking vision 107
   Snapshot: Miracle in Jersey 138

7. Rethinking guidance 140
   Snapshot: The Family Centre 158

8. Fragments and clues 160
   Final snapshot 170

   Prayer for the journey 172

   For further reading 173

   Notes 175

Caminante, no hay camino,
se hace camino al andar.

Traveller, there is no road;
the road is made by walking.

ANTONIO MACHADO, FROM PROVERBIOS Y CANTARES XXIX (1912)

1

A very personal journey

A move to the inner city

The man in the yellow hard hat looked me up and down suspiciously. 'And who might you be, then?' he asked. 'I'm the new vicar,' I replied, cheerfully. 'The rest of the family will be arriving with all our stuff in an hour or so. We're moving into the vicarage today.' He looked me up and down again. 'No you're not,' he said. 'We haven't finished building it yet.'

It was not an auspicious start to my first day as vicar of my own church. Then again, St John's Brownswood Park could never be described as an auspicious parish. Records of a wood to the north of London called Browns Wood date back to the twelfth century. By the late 19th century the place had been swallowed up by Finsbury Park, an area of urban sprawl that ended up on the edge of three London boroughs and was equally neglected by all three. The only memory of the old wood had remained in the name of the church, built between 1869 and 1878 (the delay being due to the builders going bankrupt), and a few sad-looking trees. The church was a flamboyant folly whose design was eagerly snapped up by its first vicar, George Birkett Latreille, having been rejected for Cork Cathedral. The building was large enough to seat 900. Historical records show that, by 1885, numbers attending were already in steep decline and the church was struggling to pay its way. It had been badly built and in 1928 the entire foundations had to be underpinned.

Latreille presided over a declining congregation for no less than 47 years, and most of his successors appear to have had ministries of more or less unremitting misery, sickness and depression. For decades the low numbers of worshippers meant that even essential repair works to the building were unaffordable and cracks were literally papered over. By the 1990s the church building was usable only by those who could cope with the icy cold and falling masonry, so it was closed for worship.

The immediate area had by now become a red-light district, the notorious Abu Hamza had begun to preach a violent form of Islamic radicalism at the nearby Finsbury Park Mosque, and the regular congregation of St John's had fallen below ten. On Sunday afternoons a faithful remnant met in the bar of the local Roman Catholic church for a service—an hour of genial chaos presided over by an eccentric Anglo-Catholic priest called Father Tom. The mood of gloom back at the derelict church was not helped when a dead prostitute was found in its overgrown grounds.

London Diocese decided to give the parish one last chance. Latreille's crumbling folly was finally demolished and work began to build a new St John's on the same site, along with a new vicarage. So there I stood, on 1 September 1995, inheritor of the torch of misery that was the historic lot of St John's clergy, on the doorstep of an unfinished vicarage, my family and all our belongings about to arrive at any moment. In the end, we piled our worldly goods into a side-room of the new church, in a huge heap, on the assumption that it would only be a few days till the vicarage was finished. It ended up being a month.

Needless to say, the church that became our temporary home was not finished, either. None of the doors had had locks fitted, so for several days and nights we had to wedge blocks of wood under them to keep them shut—including the main church doors. One morning we awoke to the sight of a thick-set man with a long scar across his cheek, pushing into our temporary bedroom in search of food. Our belongings were covered in a fine layer of builders' dust.

We washed our two small children in the sparkling new church kitchen sink before we took them down the road to start at their new schools.

Towards the end of our month living in the church, the congregation decided to hold a Community Festival to celebrate the opening of their new premises. The obvious drawback to this plan was that the building to be opened to curious (and, in some cases, frankly dysfunctional) neighbours was the place where we were still living. Our concerns were overruled, and the family was duly volunteered to run the hook-a-duck stall.

By 9am the locals had begun to arrive and poke around the new church, most of them ignoring the signs warning them to keep out of the hall where we were living. At this point, after a month of frustration, my wife decided she couldn't take any more. She grabbed our children, ran down the road to Finsbury Park station and boarded the first train to somewhere clean and orderly, which turned out to be Welwyn Garden City. I spent the rest of the day sitting by myself beside a paddling pool full of rubber ducks, slightly dazed and wondering what had happened to my life. As I recall, nobody asked me what had happened to my family—who did return later that same evening!

The disappearing box

Sometimes leaders are forced to think outside the box because the box has been taken away. Sometimes creativity is forced by circumstances.

Over the next six years I had to throw away any strategies I thought I had for successful ministry. Inspirational books on church leadership sat unopened on the bookshelves of the new vicarage because none of them bore any relation to what I was experiencing. The conferences I attended were hilariously irrelevant, particularly those run by large and thriving churches who encouraged us to bring our 'team' for training and inspiration. Most of the clergy attending these conferences had paid staff teams and home-groups far larger than my entire congregation. I had to think fresh thoughts, dream new dreams, rethink who I was and what God might be calling me to do and generally throw caution to the wind.

My curacy in a middle-sized, middle-class, suburban evangelical church in Ealing had scarcely prepared me for ministry in a tiny, struggling, multi-ethnic, Anglo-Catholic mission church in the inner city, so I was forced to improvise. But improvisation does not mean making everything up from scratch: it involves taking existing elements and trying to combine them in creative ways. A jazz saxophonist or rock lead guitarist uses the notes of a given scale (such as the blues scale), over a chord progression played by a group of fellow musicians who all add their own distinctives. In Brownswood Park my challenge was to improvise using my own prior experiences, ideas and evangelical emphases, over a backing of Anglican parish responsibilities and St John's Anglo-Catholicism, along with a small band of existing church members, most of them hailing originally from the Caribbean island of Montserrat—and we did it in the context of a particular inner-city community. If any one of those elements had been different, the result would have been quite different too. Of course, the results of all this improvisation might have been a creative fusion or a jarring cacophony; we would not know until we started.

My six years in Brownswood Park were by turns exhausting, challenging and inspiring. As so often happens, it took disorientation to generate creativity. I had always believed that creativity was a good thing; I had been involved in the arts and media and written a book of Christian perspectives on the fashion industry.[1] But it took the move to Brownswood Park to force me to realise that it is possible to think outside the box in terms of church leadership. In Brownswood Park there was no box. There was no default setting, no successful ecclesiastical franchise to sustain, no script to follow, no leadership team, no resources, barely even a congregation. All I had was an unfinished, empty church building, a few fixed reference points and a nagging sense that God had called me there for a reason.

A couple of years into my time in Brownswood Park, I wrote a book called *Restoring the Wonder*.[2] It was presented as a book to help people rediscover the wonder of their daily lives. Behind the scenes, this was a self-help book in a very literal sense. It was my own attempt to come to terms with where I had ended up, an attempt to find the unique wonder of this strange new place that was now our home but was outwardly so unappealing. And it was an attempt to rediscover the wonder of my own call to minister in that sort of area.

I remember thinking at the time, 'Wouldn't it be great if all church leaders had to think outside the box and improvise? Wouldn't it be great if we didn't rely on other people's models of church, as if the success of a church in California, Seoul or central London could be replicated in our own context if only we followed their formula closely enough? Wouldn't it be great if every church leader felt called to develop a unique and creative ministry in the particular place they are called to serve? Wouldn't it be great if all church leaders felt able to be creative, whatever the setting of their ministry?'

A change of parish

After six years in Brownswood Park we moved to the Strawberry Hill area of Twickenham, west London, to the parish of Holy Trinity. Culturally, Twickenham could not have been more different from the inner city. Holy Trinity looks out across Twickenham Green, a traditional English village green with cricket pavilion, park benches and young families with golden labradors and frisbees. Strawberry

Hill has few of the visible social problems of an area such as Brownswood Park. In many ways, however, the problems of Holy Trinity ran even deeper than those of St John's. Numbers attending services were disastrously low. The reputation of the church among the community was nearing rock bottom. Change would clearly be needed.

Early in my time at Holy Trinity, I sat discussing its problems and opportunities, and my own role there, with a clergy colleague. In particular, we were discussing the obvious need for a major rethink. During the conversation she asked me, 'So what's the blueprint? What's your vision for what the church will look like in ten years' time?' I realised I couldn't answer. In fact, I felt uneasy with the question itself, but at the time I struggled to say why. After all, she was describing the normal process of visionary leadership: the ability of a leader to see a better future and help others reach it. The more I thought about it, the more I realised that I felt uneasy about the word 'blueprint'. My colleague's question was, in effect, 'In ten years' time, will this church look like Brompton or Bishopsgate, Willow Creek or Saddleback? Will it be cell-church, seeker-sensitive, New Wine, Reform, or Forward in Faith? Which vision of church are you borrowing for Strawberry Hill?'

It is a natural question to ask a church leader who wants to help turn around a flagging church. There is a widespread expectation, among the public at large and among clergy themselves, that church leaders will essentially be guardians. It is assumed that a primary role of the clergy is to guard an existing church tradition or guard a new formula for how to build a successful church. Despite these popular expectations, there is good reason to question a guardianship model of ministry. It encourages people to find ready-made, pre-packaged answers rather than asking hard questions about what creative and distinctive ministry could look like in their own local context.

The peril of standardisation

Back in 1926, Europe was still recovering from World War I. The essayist and novelist G.K. Chesterton stared pessimistically into the future, commenting, 'There is nothing in front but a flat wilderness of standardisation either by Bolshevism or Big Business'.[3] Today we could be forgiven for staring into the future of the church and seeing more or less what Chesterton saw: a flat wilderness of standardised churches, created by guardians of either established traditions or new formulas, one type driven by inflexible and centrally dictated norms, the other by free-market cloning.

Any model of ministry which assumes that the church leader is primarily a guardian of a tried-and-tested tradition or a new formula tends to exclude the locally specific, the original and the idiosyncratic. In a guardianship model, all the reference points for a church lie outside itself, in a standardised format given by a wider tradition, training manual or current fad; there is little scope for asking God to help shape a unique, creative church in a particular context in a way that has integrity.

For me, the issue was crystallised during my time in Twickenham. A high-profile American evangelical church set up a branch in the town, offering exactly the same format of service, music and Bible teaching as they offered back home in the States, which had exactly the same mix as their central London congregation and their other congregations across Europe. There was no consultation with the existing churches of Twickenham about whether there was a need for the American style of service, or whether something similar was already being offered in one or more of the local churches. There was no hint of reflection that their energies might be more profitably spent in supporting the mission of another local church. Nor did the church leadership do any particular homework on the culture of the west London suburbs and tailor their approach accordingly.

Nobody could doubt the zeal and sincerity of this church: they were driven by a genuine desire to engage in Christian mission to our community. But the contours of that mission were similar to those of a coffee-shop franchise, and the profile of its leadership to that of a franchisee. It seemed to me to be a restricted and unhealthy vision for a church and its leadership. It all left me feeling rather unsettled.

The question underlying this book is: 'What if we were to see the role of church leader not so much as the guardian of a tradition or formula, but as an *explorer*, a creative person who takes people on a journey of discovery and opens up fresh possibilities?' The explorer is somebody who heads off on a journey with others, for the sheer excitement of travelling and the wonder of arriving at new places not seen before. How can this sort of leader possibly know in advance precisely what the journey will look like or where it will take them?

No roads

This model for church leadership echoes the Spanish poet Antonio Machado, quoted at the start of this book. There is no road, he says; we make the road by walking. Machado's image is of a traveller venturing into new, uncharted territory. Explorers cannot expect to find a well-surfaced and clearly marked road waiting for them. They are called to make new roads, appropriate to the landscape in which they find themselves. They are called to be creative and to improvise with what is to hand. When a new leader starts work in a church, this new combination has never existed before: this unique leader, in this unique church, in this unique community, at this unique moment in history. The call to leadership is a call to an adventure of creativity in a unique context.

The image of leader as explorer might sound like a recipe for endless novelty, for a church constantly journeying beyond familiar reference points. That would, however, be a misunderstanding. The explorer is a person who not only discovers new places and builds new roads, but also one who uncovers ancient roads and follows ancient wisdom for how to travel well. In a culture of novelty and trivia, the true explorer is likely to be a rediscoverer of neglected traditions and forgotten places.

A conversation

The origins of this book lie in my own experience of leading four Anglican churches in the London area over nearly 20 years, and the book was finished as I began a new phase of ministry centred on a market town in mid-Wales. The London parishes were in very diverse settings: two in posh suburbia, two in the inner city; of these, two were white-majority churches and two multi-ethnic. Their churchmanship traditions were a wide mix, including evangelical (with a significant component of post-evangelical), Anglo-Catholic, central/liberal and charismatic. This is not to mention the years my wife and I spent in a team of four small village churches in rural Cambridgeshire before my ordination, plus the experience of my own Methodist childhood. If nothing else, this magical mystery tour of church traditions and settings gives me a bit of confidence to write about each as an insider, rather than as an unsympathetic heckler from the margins.

In addition, this book is based on the experiences of other church leaders in different parts of the UK. I have included a series of 'Snapshots' between chapters, drawn from very diverse settings and church traditions. These snapshots are not intended particularly to illustrate the specific points made in the preceding chapter; rather, I feel that each one embodies the kind of creative, unique, locally specific approach to ministry I have in mind.

The book has been born, in part, out of frustration at the dominance of standardised models of successful church leadership on offer in theological colleges, books, conferences and courses, and in the minds of many church leaders themselves. So, in a sense, this is a very personal journey. It is made all the more personal because this is the sort of book I wish somebody had given me as I started out in my first parish. In all these years, nobody else has written that book, so I decided it was time to have a go myself.

Nevertheless, I aspire to be more than Narcissus gazing at his own reflection in a pool. I hope the book will connect with people from a broad range of church traditions, and with a number of important wider conversations in today's church.

Writings on creative leadership

Recent years have seen a significant growth in the number of books on church leadership, mirroring the expanding market for books on business leadership. But few of these books, manuals and courses have highlighted creativity or the ability to improvise as essential characteristics or skills. Until as recently as the start of the 21st century, almost no books on church leadership so much as mentioned creativity or the desirability of shaping a unique and creative church, or even dealt with these issues under alternative headings, such as 'inventiveness' or 'originality'. This in itself raises interesting questions about why church leadership and creativity have not usually been bracketed together—an issue that we shall explore. Around the turn of the millennium, a small number of church leadership books began the call for creativity, notably those by Leonard Sweet and Erwin McManus.[4] *Ministry Rediscovered* is, in part, a conversation with those books.

Emerging church

Recent years have seen an explosion of attempts to rethink church for a new generation. Many theorists, including John Drane and Brian McLaren, have been speaking in terms of engaging with postmodern culture.[5] In some cases the debate is framed in terms of the church's adaptation to the world of post-Christendom.[6] In the USA it has been framed in terms of 'emerging' or 'emergent' churches, although in practice this label tends to be reserved for a particular style of self-consciously 'cool', culturally aware, experimental church.

This is not a book about how to lead an emerging church, although I was privileged to help found *Grace*, one of the first emerging worship communities in the UK. Most of the discussion about emerging church has been taking place between consenting adults, people with a shared distaste for 'traditional' church, or those who have dropped out of the mainstream church due to bad experiences. So the details of the emergent conversation have bypassed most churches. But the conversation about creative leadership of creative churches is too important to remain as the sole preserve of those drawn to arty and experimental forms of worship. It ought to have repercussions for all church leaders, from Father Dominic at the Oratory to Pastor Ezekiel at Springs of Life Fellowship, to Reverend Green of Little Bumbling Parish Church. I hope this book may be a conversation with these colleagues, too, since my main concern here is with the inherited church out of which the emergents are emerging. The injection of creativity into all our churches seems, to me, a bigger and more interesting challenge than launching little lifeboats of creativity while the grand old liner slowly disappears below the waves. So this book draws on some of the themes I was exploring some years back with the team who set up *Grace*—themes that continue to be explored by those pioneering new styles of church today[7]—but it aims to apply these themes to the church in its inherited mode.

Fresh Expressions and Missional Church

In the UK there has been an exciting rise in 'fresh expressions' of church, particularly in the Church of England and Methodist Church. They follow in the wake of the seminal *Mission-Shaped*

Church report of 2004[8] and subsequent *Expressions* DVDs, which recognised the general failure of most churches to connect with the majority of people in contemporary British and European culture, and called for priority to be given to planting new styles of church aimed at particular networks. The 'fresh expressions' label tends to cover a broader range of pioneering Christian communities than the 'emerging' label, and might include anything from targeted meetings for toddlers or the elderly to a small rural parish integrating worship with country walks. Key movers in Fresh Expressions have been the Anglican Bishops Graham Cray and Steven Croft.

There has been a parallel and significant development in the USA for 'Missional' churches. Its principal inspiration was the British missionary Bishop Lesslie Newbigin, who returned home in 1974 after spending most of his working life in India, only to find that Britain itself had become a post-Christian culture requiring a missionary encounter of its own. The Missional Church movement calls on all Christians and churches to have a missionary approach to their own culture. Consequently, words such as 'inculturation' and 'contextualisation' have a particular resonance for missional church leaders. Spokespeople include the Canadian church consultant and former pastor Alan Roxburgh, whose writing has been a major influence on my own ministry and some of the themes in this book.[9]

This is a rapidly evolving area for today's church, but at the time of writing there is a significant overlap between the goals of emerging church, fresh expressions and missional church. Each aims to help shape a church that engages creatively with contemporary culture, and various descriptive terms are used with different nuances by different groups. Perhaps the main difference is that fresh expressions and missional churches are both essentially about a missionary approach to their host culture. They are fundamentally about outreach. Emerging church, on the other hand, is primarily concerned with the renewal of church culture itself. It is about creating culturally aware communities with culturally appropriate theology and worship styles. So an emerging church might well be full of Christians, jaded and disillusioned with the worship styles and theologies in which they were brought up. That could be sufficient reason for its existence, while a missional church or fresh expression exists almost entirely for non-members. The absence of an effective missional focus would remove its *raison d'être* entirely.

The thesis of this book draws significantly from the emphasis in both Fresh Expressions and Missional Church on incarnating the gospel in a particular local culture. But it perhaps has more in common with the missional approach than with the fresh expressions, in that it hopes to help transform 'mainstream' churches as a whole, rather than adding creative outreach projects on to a largely unchanged parent church.

Christianity Rediscovered

The title of my book contains a deliberate echo of Vincent Donovan's classic text on Christian mission, *Christianity Rediscovered*.[10] Donovan was a Catholic missionary to the Masai of East Africa in the 1960s. He found that, after a century of mission to Masai, the missionaries had accumulated all the paraphernalia of missions (schools, buildings, mission compounds) but had still seen no converts. He began to wonder if part of the problem was that they had simply imported a Western version of the faith, naively assuming it to be universally valid, along with unchallenged and wooden assumptions about the way missions had to be carried out. He found that he had to lay these assumptions aside and enter the culture of the Masai, on their terms: 'I have no theory, no plan, no strategy, no gimmicks, no idea of what will come.'[11]

In the preface to the second edition of his book, Donovan cites a perceptive comment from an American priest that, although the book is set in East Africa, it is really about the church in Europe and the US. Donovan does not explore this idea further, beyond noting that youth culture in the US was becoming every bit as tribal as the Masai, and expressing a hope that others would develop and apply his ideas in contexts where he could not.

My echo of Donovan's title does not amount to a claim that this book will prove equally original, pioneering or provocative. There is, however, a basic similarity of approach to Donovan's: a desire to pull together a specific cultural context with the heart of the Christian message, 'to see what emerges if anything can emerge, without knowing what the end result will be'.[12] In particular, this book underlines Donovan's concern that we must not pretend to know the final destination before the journey of exploration even begins. I hope that, in some small way, this book might similarly give a few other church leaders the courage to question the monolithic assumptions endemic in so many churches and traditions and to discover the joys of exploration.

Low-key creatives today

Up and down the land today, there are many unsung church leaders exercising creative ministries in low-key, unspectacular ways—such as those described in my 'Snapshots' between chapters. Some leaders are pioneering new and unique ways to connect with the sceptical and indifferent members of their local communities. Some are stirring the pot of churchmanship and emerging with fresh combinations. Some opt to work in a region of the country or sector of society where they are out of their own comfort zone for the sake of mission. In my opinion, these low-key creatives are the true heroes of the contemporary church scene; but, in my experience, many of them feel isolated and out on a limb. One of the perils of stepping out from the crowd is that you lose the reassuring sense of safety in numbers.

Let me give just one example, among many. Over the years I have known a number of evangelical leaders ministering in non-evangelical churches, without a like-minded staff team and, in some cases, without a single like-minded church member. Their work is often inspirational, going with the grain of a local church's tradition but enriching it with their own evangelical emphases—such as a serious engagement with scripture, the centrality of the cross, and a call to a faith that touches the heart. In missional terms, this can be hugely effective. These churches are often well equipped to appeal to their local communities because they can feel less daunting or 'full-on' than churches with a standard evangelical package. Their worship can be more accessible to people with a church background from childhood, because they retain recognisable elements such as traditional hymns and liturgy.

One consequence of such a pioneering ministry, though, can be that the leaders spend much of their working lives feeling lonely and stretched to the limit. This can be made worse by suspicion from fellow evangelicals who assume that they are not quite 'kosher' (why else would they have chosen to minister in a high church or liberal setting?), and suspicion from self-appointed guardians of tradition in the church they lead, because they don't appear to buy the whole of that package either: they seem suspiciously prone to talking about the need for change. These are ministries that can look messy to outsiders, often feel frustrating to practitioners and can't be reduced to an easy slogan. The reality—that these are leaders at the cutting edge of mission—rarely seems to be recognised and celebrated.

One of the bestselling US books on creative church leadership is by Ed Young, pastor of a megachurch of over 20,000 members on a 141-acre campus in the Dallas/Fort Worth area of Texas.[13] One of his examples of creativity in worship involves the curtains of his auditorium being opened at the beginning of a service to reveal a full-size British Scorpion tank onstage. The pastor then begins his address from inside the tank via a live link. There is no faulting Young's creative ingenuity, but the uniqueness and creativity I have in mind has little to do with Cecil B. DeMille sermon illustrations. It has more to do with out-of-the-box leadership on a shoestring, carried out in ordinary settings and often scarcely noticed. I hope this book can be part of a conversation that encourages heroic low-key creatives to realise that what they are doing is valuable beyond measure, and encourages others to join them.

I also hope it will help fellow church leaders to resist the lure of the 'guardian of tradition' mentality which has taken hold in churches of all types and is the subject of the next chapter.

2

Cloning the church

Tescopoly

For most of the 'noughties' (2001–2009) I lived with my family in Twickenham, best known as the home of English rugby. During this time we witnessed dramatic changes to the character of the town centre. When we first arrived, one of the attractions of the area was its wide range of local stores, including two butchers, a number of greengrocers and independently owned coffee shops. The butcher down the road from us knew his customers well and had a repertoire of dry, humorous retorts. I once asked if he had leg of lamb. He solemnly replied, 'No, mate, I always stand like this.' Most of the coffee shops, too, were locally owned and run. One in particular was like a small community centre, where the proprietor would not only serve coffee but would also ask after people's grandchildren and cousins by name. She functioned not only as a barrista but as a pastor.

By the time we left Twickenham, these small butchers, grocers and locally owned coffee shops had almost all gone, forced out of business by declining trade. Just one greengrocer remained in the centre of the town and his future looked uncertain. There were a number of reasons why this happened. The most significant was the arrival of a Tesco megastore. In the early 1990s, a huge new Tesco opened on the site of a former hospital, close to Twickenham rugby stadium. By 2006, more than half of all grocery shopping in Twickenham was being done in Tesco.[1] Even the live music venue close to our old home became a Tesco Local store.

Across the UK, Tesco controls fully one-third of all spending on groceries. The big four supermarket chains, Tesco, Sainsbury's, Asda and Morrison's, between them account for more than three-quarters of the UK grocery market: 75.6 per cent. With more than £3 billion of profits on sales of nearly £60 billion annually (2009 figures), Tesco has managed to become the dominant player in UK retail. The appeal of Tesco to customers is obvious. It has a strong brand identity and offers people what they want: a vast selection of goods at low prices. It is fast and convenient, predictable and risk-free. Whichever store you visit, your shopping experience will be reassuringly familiar and predictably affordable and will add to your tally of Clubcard loyalty points.

Essential to the rise of supermarkets such as Tesco is convenience and predictability for the consumer, and reproducibility for the company. Consumers have to be able to access the same product lines, at the same price, in the same ambience. You have to give the people what they have come to expect from the brand. Leadership in Tesco is about learning the history of the brand, what makes it so effective, and how to replicate the model. So trainee leaders are immersed in the ethos of the brand and carefully trained up in exactly the right way of doing things to ensure uniformity of product and service.

Whether new managers are training for leadership in Tesco or Starbucks, Disney or Coca-Cola, they are instilled with a passion for the personality of the brand and sent forth to multiply in an aggressive policy of expansion.[2]

Local shops and hedgerows

The main casualties of this relentless cloning and homogenisation are the local and particular, the eccentric and specific. Smaller local stores that have built up their business over many decades or even centuries, to respond to the needs of a local community, may end up being forced out of business. Skills handed on over generations may be lost, along with the personal touch. Surveys reveal that, on average, local shopkeepers know seven out of ten of their customers personally.

The rise of megastores has hit small local shops hard. Across the UK, specialist local shops such as butchers, bakers and fish-mongers have been closing at the astonishing rate of 50 a week.[3] We recently visited an area of rural Suffolk where my wife had lived as a teenager. We wanted to buy cartons of drink, so we went in search of the local stores she remembered from years ago. But there were no longer any such shops there: they had all closed. During the decade 2000–2010, around 7000 small and independent shops closed in London and, at the time of writing, were still closing at a rate of 1000 a year.[4]

This has been a national tragedy, all the more tragic because the happy supermarket shoppers loading up the boots of their cars have been either unaware of the decimation of a vast ecology of local livelihoods or indifferent to it.

There has been a parallel loss in Britain's native countryside hedgerows, particularly in the eastern counties of England. These ancient hedgerows have historically supported a vast range of wildlife, including more than 600 plant species, 1500 insects, 65 birds and 20 mammals. They are the main home for no less than 47 species threatened with extinction. Since World War II, 186,000 miles of Britain's ancient hedgerows have been destroyed, along with 95 per cent of our wildflower meadows, half of our chalk grasslands and half our wetlands.[5]

True, some new hedges have been planted too. But a new hedgerow cannot replace the historical, ecological and aesthetic significance of a hedge that is centuries old. Each ancient hedgerow is a unique ecosystem, specific and native to its local area. Each is irreplaceable.

Does it matter? Should we not just accept that time moves on, the world changes and new patterns of retail and ecology emerge that are better suited to the world of today? Clearly, that must be the view of the majority. How else to explain the relentless planting of Tescos and uprooting of ancient hedges? Still, any reader who is unmoved at the thought of 50 specialist local shops a week closing down, and thousands of miles of unique hedgerow being uprooted every year, is unlikely to be convinced by the rest of this book. It is an extended plea for a rediscovery of the value of local and particular, the eccentric and specific in our churches. It is a plea for uniqueness.

Tesco churches

Uniqueness and unpredictability ought to be second nature to all our churches. After all, we worship a God who delights in uniqueness, from our own irises and fingerprints to snowflakes and planets. Churches in denominations with a parish system, such as the Church of England and the Church in Wales, ought to have uniqueness and unpredictability built into the way they do church: mission to a designated patch of our nation has been uniquely designated to us.

Most of us, though, have lost our nerve. Especially in urban areas, the parish system has largely fallen into neglect, except in the case of legal formalities such as marriage law. It has been commonplace at the livelier, more forward-looking end of the church to pour scorn on the parish system as an anachronism and obstacle to growth. Bishop David Pytches, best known for his pioneering charismatic ministry at St Andrew's Chorleywood and as founder of the New Wine conferences, has been quoted as describing the parish system as 'the condom of the Church of England', since he believed it prevented natural growth and reproduction.

For several decades, church leaders of all traditions have been staring into the blindingly obvious and either not seeing it or re-fusing to acknowledge it. Let me say it again: our churches are all in unique settings, each with a unique group of people, living at a unique time in history. Those of us entrusted with care of a parish have a special mandate for mission to that parish. Instead, too many of us have preferred to follow a Tesco strategy of homogenisation and convenience.[6] We have become guardians of a recognised and familiar tradition, rather than explorers.

The instinct to be a guardian of a wider tradition in the church is a noble one: we wish to preserve and protect something that we recognise to be of value. We guard because we care. The drawback of being a guardian of any church tradition, however, is that we can be overprotective and inflexible, so set on guarding what we have that we neglect to explore new possibilities, or fail to respond to the variables of a local community.

The prolific inventor Thomas Edison (1847–1931), best known for his pioneering work on the electric light bulb, had a unique way of recruiting his assistants. He would invite them over for a lunch that included a bowl of soup. If the candidate automatically shook salt or pepper in the soup before tasting it, they instantly failed the interview. Edison wanted his assistants to be open-minded types who would respond to the facts as they found them (did the soup actually need more salt, or was it already too salty?), rather than approaching a task with fixed assumptions already in place. (I always shake salt over my soup.) A guardianship model of church leadership is one that 'knows' in advance of tasting the soup that it will need salt and pepper shaken over it, because all soups do. Or perhaps it knows in advance that the soup will need salt and pepper, because a wonderful soup it once tasted in Shrewsbury or Seattle did.

Guarding the tradition

For many church leaders, the primary tradition they guard is that of their denomination. For others it is a broader tradition that crosses denominational labels. Within my own Anglican tradition, more leaders derive a sense of identity from their particular wing of the church than they do from any shared sense of Anglican identity. Many Anglican churches have more in common with like-minded churches of other denominations than they do with the parish church next door. We tend to be network-tribal.

But this urge to guard the distinctives of a particular denomination or tradition comes carrying heavy luggage. The tradition we guard so assiduously will include expectations about the style of worship (a hymn-sandwich using traditional hymns; or half an hour of contemporary soft-rock to start the service; or a performance by a professional robed choir; or ambient music on CD), and it will include expectations about the talk (a ten-minute homily on items in the news; or an hour-long expository sermon on a Bible passage; or interactive chat with visual aids), and so on. Each tradition tends to come loaded with its own approaches to the aesthetics of worship space, mission, the place of the sacraments (or not), dress in church, its own way of praying, its own terms for unbelievers, and its own set of clichés. Each has its own historic centres of excellence and gatherings where identity and values are reinforced, and each has its own strictly delineated boundary fences.

Vast sections of global Christianity more or less assume a guardian-of-tradition model of ministry. The word 'catholic', after all, means 'universal', and Roman Catholic means the universal church as defined by Rome. It is a matter of pride to traditional Catholicism that it aspires to a uniform model of priesthood and liturgy wherever it is to be found. Many Catholics still bemoan the loss of the Latin Mass for the very reason of its universality. To take another example, the word 'orthodoxy' comes from the Greek for 'having the right opinion', meaning an adherence to the traditional and accepted in matters of faith. In Eastern Orthodox churches, this idea is extended not only to the core doctrines of faith but also to their outward expression. Innovation equals apostasy. So the traditions of icon painting become fixed and not subject to revision or individual interpretation. Individuality and innovation are seen as problematic, stasis and changelessness as an ideal. Liturgy and patterns of priesthood, too, have become fixed across centuries of tradition. So the two oldest strands of Christianity, Catholicism and Orthodoxy, both define themselves in significant measure by their resistance to originality, innovation or uniqueness.

Similarly, the Anglican Church has historically tended to define itself in opposition to innovation or extremes. Its origins lie in the turbulent politics of 16th-century England and an attempt to found a state church that avoided the perceived extremes of Roman Catholicism and Calvinism. For this reason, Anglican apologists have spoken warmly of charting a *via media*, or middle way, between two extremes. The desire for a church to have a coherent identity is a laudable one. In practice, however, the Church of England in particular has all too often ended up driving slowly down the middle of the road. Anglicanism's history of welcoming innovation and fresh ideas has not, until recently, been a good one. Perhaps the most glaring example of this is the Anglican Church's inability to welcome and harness the vision and energy of the Methodist revival in the 18th century. What hope was there for creative, visionary types in a church where the most damning term of abuse from their fellow clergy was 'enthusiast', and where the revival's rediscovery of the biblical themes of new birth, justification by faith and the work of the Holy Spirit in a believer were seen as a dangerous whipping-up of the feeble-minded?

Guardians of tradition do not only preside over historic churches that prize antiquity, changelessness or a *via media*. They are just as likely to preside over Pentecostal, charismatic, hip youth con-gregations and socially aware liberal churches. Traditions can be new and noisy as well as old and quiet. Guardians of tradition are the church leaders who aspire to being the church equivalent of Tesco managers: a safe pair of hands, competent stewards of an existing model (new or old) which looks more or less the same wherever it is to be found.

Having said this, of course every church needs roots, a sense of history and a connection to the doctrines and practices of the wider Church. One of the hallmarks of creative churches today is a fresh willingness to engage with tradition. But a monolithic tradition of any variety can become a straitjacket. A desire to guard and defend a tradition can blind us to the real challenge, which is contextualising the gospel and the tradition we inherit in a way that is authentic for our own unique place, with our own unique people, at our own unique moment in history. Learning a guardianship style of leadership is essentially about learning to sustain an existing brand, and there will be an expectation from the denomination, network or tradition that its leaders will police the boundary fence. Leaders are expected to be guardians of their particular slice of the grand tradition, rather than custodians of the whole lot.

Guarding the new idea

While some church leaders are guardians of a denomination or worship tradition, others guard a specific formula or programme that has been successful elsewhere. These leaders tend to be conference addicts, with one eye on their home church, the other scanning the horizon for the arrival of the US Cavalry to save the day.

The past 30 years or so have seen the rise of a number of new, dynamic and creative churches, particularly in America. These include Willow Creek in Chicago, under the inspirational leadership of Bill Hybels, and California's Saddleback under Rick Warren, internationally known for his 'Purpose Driven' series of books. Willow Creek and Saddleback are merely the most visible tip of a booming industry of conferences, training days, books, resource packs, DVDs, CDs and podcasts. A large number of Stateside churches are developing models of ministry that are being eagerly consumed around the world.

The US megachurches like to present themselves as great laboratories of the Spirit (to borrow a phrase from Welsh poet R.S. Thomas), places with the personnel and resources to try out new ideas and share their findings with more hard-pressed, busy and less well-resourced church leaders. They see themselves as centres for experimentation, trying out exciting new ways of doing worship, mission or discipleship to find out what works, saving the rest of us the time, effort and outlay. The results are then packaged for easy consumption.

The irony, however, is that the US megachurches have rarely been offering at conferences what they experienced themselves. They sell a programme, when what they experienced was a process or journey.

From journey to programme

Bill Hybels is a creative leader. Read the story of the origins of Willow Creek[7] or listen to the personal stories woven through his talks, and you find the inspirational story of a man driven by frustration at the failings of the church of his childhood; a man tireless in exploring creative ways to reconnect the Christian faith with the culture of suburban Chicago. It is a story of developing a unique church in creative ways. We may not like everything Willow Creek does or represents, but there is no doubting its desire for creativity and originality.

Many Americans can be characterised as loving programmes and success formulas, with a love that they have exported to church leaders around the world. Before long, there was a steady stream of pilgrims eager to learn from Willow Creek how to implement its successful 'seeker-sensitive' model of ministry. Large-scale conferences were held across the globe, sharing the Willow Creek blueprint for growth. Similarly, Saddleback exported Rick Warren's

'Purpose-Driven Church' model as a blueprint for others to follow. Toronto Airport Christian Fellowship led conferences where guests could experience John Arnott's 'Toronto blessing' approach to ministry and learn how to reproduce it back home. In recent years, church leaders have flocked to conferences to learn from Bill Johnson about the healing ministry and focus on the miraculous at his Bethel Church in Redding, California, or to hear Mike and Cindy Riches from Tacoma in the USA's Pacific Northwest expound the principles of their 'Jesus ministry'.

Something is lost, however, when a unique local journey is packaged into a conference and rolled up into a blueprint. Something is lost when a distinctive story is told and others then try to make it their own, in the process implicitly dismissing their own story as somehow less glamorous or worthwhile.

I remember overhearing a conversation at an early Purpose-Driven Church conference between two British delegates who were members of Rick Warren's Purpose-Driven network. They were sharing stories about their successes and failures in implementing in their own churches every detail of the pattern that had had such success at Saddleback and was outlined in Warren's *Purpose-Driven Church* book. Specifically, they were comparing notes on where different people in their churches were on Warren's 'baseball diamond' model of life development. They clearly believed that the model had to be followed exactly. It seemed to me a rather sad conversation. All that energy directed into searching out answers from California, that could more profitably have gone into looking at the world on their own doorstep and asking God for fresh eyes to see what was going on around them! All that effort to transplant a Californian Redwood into a suburban English garden!

It would be genuinely helpful to hear the pioneers of successful megachurches admit, 'It's not about me and my journey. It's about you and your journey. This is how I was creative in my own context. How are you going to be creative in yours?' This may be what some of these inspirational leaders hope they are doing, but, from years of attending these conferences and chatting to other delegates, I can say with some confidence that this is not what most delegates are after. Most want a tried-and-tested solution to their problems, stamped 'Made in America'.

Those who attend conferences in search of fresh inspiration might be surprised to hear themselves described as guardians. The word implies defensiveness, while they are more likely to see themselves as being on the cutting edge of mission and worship. The irony is that it is as easy to become defensive and inflexible about a new, imported model of church as about the most traditional of models. A guardian mentality always cares more about defending the purity of the model and applying it 'correctly' than about asking hard questions relating to the creative and distinctive ministry that God might want us to develop in our own setting.

Entrepreneurial spirit

There is another dimension to the Americanisation of church strategy. Americans not only tend to love programmes and success formulas; they also love entrepreneurs and motivational gurus. In the church scene, this has been seen in the dramatic increase in personal ministries with a specific focus. The process usually starts when a Christian pastor or author writes on a subject close to their heart or from their own experience. This results in invitations to speak at churches and conferences on the theme of the book. Before long, the author has a particular ministry and is featured on Christian TV and radio, talking about that ministry. When they speak at conferences or in churches, their reputation goes before them: they become famous as 'X who was abused by her father but found a loving heavenly Father', 'Y who has had encounters with angels' or 'Z who teaches the God-given laws of success and prosperity'.

These speakers have little reason to encourage their hearers to shape a unique and creative church. A motivational Christian speaker with a niche reputation and a family and ministry team to support is unlikely to say to an adoring disciple, 'Frankly, the ministry I'm offering is the last thing you need in your church.' Their role is simple. It is to diagnose a very specific problem, which churches may or may not know they have: for example, that lots of Christian women have a warped image of God because their own father was abusive or distant; or that most Christians have never met an angel; or that most Christians are poor because they don't realise God wants them rich and successful. Then they offer their own solution to this problem. This usually involves the disciple in buying the speaker's books and DVDs, joining a mailing list and inviting the speaker to lead a day-conference on the topic at their church to rectify the perceived problem.

The result is another network of conferences and products offering standard solutions to local and complex problems; offering a blueprint when what is needed is a journey; offering easy answers when what is needed is help in asking the right questions. Then again, why would a Peugeot salesman tell you that the car you really need is made by VW?

Soon after we moved from Twickenham to Kennington in south London, I realised there was no house number outside our home, which meant that visitors and even postal delivery people struggled to identify the place where we lived as number 56. So I went to a local hardware store and asked whether they had house numbers for sale. The man behind the counter looked at me thoughtfully. 'I do,' he said, 'if you live at number 27', and he showed me the evidence: his total stock of house numbers was one small metal plaque bearing the number 27.

All too often, church growth conferences have been hardware stores selling one house number. It is, of course, possible that you will be one of the few lucky customers whose home address fits the number they are selling, but it's unlikely. That leaves two options:

you can move house to number 27 and buy the plaque the shop is selling, or you can embark on a search for the right number for the home where you actually live.

Church planting as cloning

Most church planting is done by energetic, enthusiastic people fired up by faith, but all too often their vision is limited to reproducing the culture of the sending church because they are convinced that it is the 'right' way to do things and they have seen God at work there. It is one of the ironies of the contemporary church that some of the most dynamic church planters are the least committed to creativity and uniqueness. At a recent church planting conference in London, a representative from a large and popular church spoke of their ambition to produce an 'out-of-the-box' (as opposed to an 'outside-the-box') resource for church planters. They wanted to offer a one-size-fits-all pack that would give a simple and detailed blueprint for any large church, anywhere in the UK, to plant a daughter church. This is not so much church planting as church cloning.

There is, however, another model for church planting—one that requires time, patience and a painstaking process of dialogue and contextualisation involving the host church and its surrounding culture.[8] This is a 'road less travelled' because it is slower and harder.

Even (heaven help us) fresh expressions and emerging churches can miss the point, ending up predictable and going through the motions. One of the most depressing services I have attended was in the early days of experimental alternative worship. The service turned out to be an imitation of the outward forms of new worship that the organisers had seen in other churches and at Christian festivals. It was trying hard to be cool and arty, but nobody welcomed visitors or made them feel included; there was no sense of a community of people behind the service, no sense of yearning to encounter a living God, nothing that reflected the local community. We sat in a cold, cavernous church for an hour, having ambient electronic music played at us and watching random images projected on to a sheet, then we all went home.

If we experience a fresh expression at another church, which is genuinely fresh because it grows out of fresh thinking in its own particular context, it is tempting to decide that we are going to try to reproduce it in our own, very different context. Fresh expressions and church plants are a perfect opportunity to think outside the box, but all too often they simply become a new box. Creative ministry can be carried out in any church setting, from the most traditional to the most avant-garde. So too can uncreative ministry.

A few years back, I took a three-month sabbatical from work. During that time I went with the family to visit a number of high-profile churches across the greater London area. I was shocked at the uniformity and predictability of many of the services we attended, most of which were in churches that prided themselves on being 'forward-thinking' and 'radical'. The experience left me reflecting that leaders should never feel intimidated by the size and resources of the larger, big-name churches. From all our visits, the one church that stayed in our memory was a medium-sized parish church in the suburbs, not a church most people would have heard of. The service certainly was not the most polished, or its building the most impressive. There was no great mystery as to why we liked this church best. It felt somehow real and at ease with itself; it did not feel as if it was trying to be another church.

Buses and Jeeps

The Spanish poet Machado warns the traveller that there are no roads: the only roads worth travelling are the ones we make as we go. This is an image that most church leaders would find unsettling, however. To pursue Machado's image of road travel, most church leaders aspire to being competent bus drivers. They are happy to take their people safely along a predetermined and inflexible route, with familiar stops and landmarks along the way. Few leaders aspire to being makers of new roads.

But the church of this generation desperately needs leaders who see themselves as drivers of offroad vehicles rather than buses. We need leaders who are prepared to head into uncharted terrain, especially into that least explored of all places, the world on our own doorstep. Currently, most church leaders are only using a small proportion of their potential. It's as if they are driving sturdy Jeeps designed for heavy-duty, offroad driving, but they are using them to take children to school along well-surfaced roads in well-manicured suburbs. Might it be that in our day the call of the Spirit is to a new generation of Jeep drivers, explorers who are prepared to go offroad into unexplored terrain, to make new roads and rediscover old ones?

Snapshot: From the ashes

Bankfoot is a village of a little over 1000 people, eight miles north of Perth in Scotland. For many decades the village was dominated by the tower of its 19th-century Church of Scotland parish church. Then, in February 2004, the church burned to the ground. The silverware in the church safe survived the inferno, merely blackened by the smoke, but everything else was reduced to ash.

The Revd Iain McFadzean became the new minister of this Presbyterian parish in 2005, inheriting the charred shell of the old church. At his induction social, he presented the congregation with the first item of furniture for a new church: the cracked bell that had been damaged in the fire, but had since been fashioned into a baptismal font by a cabinet-maker friend of Iain. It became a symbol of hope for the future.

Together the new minister and congregation drew up plans for a new church. A crucial factor in the redevelopment was the historic lack of good leisure, social and medical facilities for its rural community. From day one, the phrase that guided the rebuilding was 'Bankfoot Church and Community Building Together', with a dream of a building that would become the hub of community as well as church life. It was a creative dream of worship and daily life becoming so intimately merged that there was no distinction between them.

The new Bankfoot Church Centre opened in October 2008. It not only contains a worship space, prayer room and community café, but also boasts a three-storey soft play area for toddlers, a daycare centre for elderly people, a large sports hall with shower facilities, a display area for local artists and craftspeople, and rooms to hire to local people for clubs, parties, concerts and conferences. Even the local dentist and podiatrist operate from the Bankfoot Church Centre. At the time of writing, at least 15 local organisations hold regular meetings there, including country dancing, badminton club, Boys' Brigade and Young Farmers. An electronic noticeboard advertises local trades, crafts and other businesses.

Bankfoot Church was designed with the care of the local environment in mind, situated as it is in the stunning Perthshire countryside. The church and community were determined that this had to be an eco-church, where the impact on the surrounding nature was minimal and closely monitored. The frame is made entirely from sustainable wood, the roof slates are mostly recycled, and it has one of the lowest carbon footprints for a building of its size anywhere in the UK. This is thanks to high levels of insulation and a heating system supplied by two wind generators. When there is low demand for electricity in the church centre, the surplus goes to the National Grid, generating a small amount of income for the centre. A rain water harvester takes the water that falls on the roof, stores it underground and uses it to flush toilets (a full tank can supply 3500 flushes). Even the decorative insets in the youth café are made from recycled CDs. There is a church garden and community orchard, and a small group of volunteers monitors biodiversity in the grounds.

The wooden panels near the church doors, engraved with the apostle Paul's words on the fruit of the Spirit (Galatians 5:22–23), are from an oak tree that was blown over in a storm and donated by a local farmer. Communion table, lecterns, side table and crosses are all made from the same tree. The stained glass is designed and made by a local glass works.

The church's website emphasises that the whole project emerged from listening carefully to the needs and hopes of its local community. It emerged as a disconsolate congregation, surveying the burned out remains of their church, were reminded of the words of Jeremiah 29:11: '"For I know the plans I have for you," declares the Lord, "plans to prosper you and not to harm you, plans to give you hope and a future."' This verse became the inscription on the foundation stone for the new Bankfoot Church Centre.

3

The call to creativity

Creativity-free church

In the last chapter we explored reasons why so few leaders have aspired to be shapers of creative and unique ministries in their unique churches. We saw that a guardianship model of church produces leaders who look to replicate rather than innovate or experiment. But there have also been at least five wider reasons for the general lack of creativity and willingness to think outside the box in our churches.

Suspicion of the creative arts

Historically, significant strands of the Christian Church have harboured a deep suspicion towards human creativity in general and the arts in particular. Around AD200, Tertullian set the tone in his book *De Spectaculis*. He condemned the theatre of his day because its fictional plots peddled untruths. Tertullian concluded that all the arts are the creation of demons, partly because the arts deal in immoral themes and so turn people's hearts away from God, partly because they give pleasure to the mind and senses, and so are inappropriate for believers, who should be world-denying.

Like Tertullian, many of the early Christian leaders viewed the arts and creativity through the eyes of the influential Greek philosopher Plato (428–348BC). Plato's objections to the arts were that they celebrate the 'merely' physical rather than heavenly ideals, that they pander to our baser passions rather than noble reason, and that they are nothing more than a form of play or sport, a distraction from the important business of life. One of the great figures of the early church, Augustine (354–430) praised Plato for deliberately excluding poets from his vision of utopia, and repented in his own *Confessions* of his youthful 'sin' of loving the resonant cadences in poems about ancient Troy.

The hostility of Plato and the Church Fathers to the arts has continued to resonate down the ages, particularly in relation to the popular arts. In my book on Christian approaches to fashion and the fashion industry, *Fashion & Style*, I traced the history of Christian approaches to sartorial creativity. Through the ages, fashion has been damned for a host of reasons. It has been seen as 'worldly' as opposed to 'spiritual', 'outer' as opposed to 'inner', and 'effeminate' as opposed to 'masculine'; it reflects the 'changing' as opposed to the 'unchanging', and has been seen as 'low' art rather than 'high' art (some Christians concede that forms of high art may be allowable, as they can lift the mind to higher things). In other words, from the perspective of a particular type of traditional theology, fashion finds itself on the losing side of every argument.

In reality, this body–soul dualism, which continues to afflict many quarters of the Church, is dangerously sub-Christian. It owes almost nothing to the earthy Hebrew thought patterns of the Bible but a great deal to Greek philosophy and some forms of Eastern mystical spirituality. But the damage has already been done. The stream was polluted at source, and some strands of Christianity continued to fear human creativity in general and the arts in particular, reserving special condemnation for the popular arts. They have the particular drawback of being novel and reflecting the culture of the day, which the instinctive cultural conservatism of many Christians finds especially troubling.

Fear of the image

Some Christians have historically taken the biblical ban on making 'an image in the form of anything in heaven above or on the earth beneath or in the waters below' (Exodus 20:4) to imply an absolute ban on all image-making. Consequently, some traditions of Christianity became virtually Islamic in their rejection of the image and their idealisation of the word.

The message of the second commandment is actually a warning against idolatry—shaping idols as alternatives to God. That has not stopped many in the church, such as the great reformer Calvin (1509–64), drawing from it a broader principle: that the only image to be celebrated is the image of God in human beings. Calvin memorably described human nature as a 'factory of idols'. To be fair to Calvinism, some of the leading Christian writers on art history and aesthetics have come from the more recent Dutch Neo-Calvinist tradition in Holland and North America, but many more Christians have shared with Calvin a suspicion of metaphor, allusion and representation, the basis of all art. This view has also been held by other Christians outside Calvinism.

Fear of the childish

Some Christian traditions have associated creativity and imagination with childishness, a phase to be outgrown as a person attains maturity. Most children are drawn to story and fantasy, which is generally tolerated while they are young. Those adults whose minds remain drawn to fantasy and the making of unexpected connections may be seen as somehow infantile. The words of Paul have been (mis-)quoted to bolster this view: 'When I was a child, I talked like a child, I thought like a child, I reasoned like a child. When I became a man, I put the ways of childhood behind me' (1 Corinthians 13:11). Again, it is theological nonsense to use this passage to damn imagination as infantile. In context, Paul is grasping for an apt metaphor to illustrate his argument that spiritual gifts are temporary: they are only for the current life of the church, its 'childhood', and will not be needed into eternity. Love, by contrast, never ends. It is ironic that Paul's imaginative metaphor has been used to bolster suspicion of the imagination.

Church as a refuge from change

For many people today, as in previous centuries, the church is seen primarily as a haven of changelessness in a changing world. Its predictability is its main virtue. The idea that the church might be called to engage with culture or even help to shape it is widely seen as a contradiction in terms. The church, on this view, is concerned with eternal verities, not the latest fads and fashions. In my experience, I have rarely known any group of people respond so angrily as churchgoers who see their familiar routines being subjected to change. Nor is this kind of response the preserve of just one sector of the church. For many churchgoers of all traditions, church is the one thing in life that never changes, and leaders tinker with it at their peril. A commitment to shaping a creative and locally distinctive church will be heard by some as a declaration of war, and many church leaders bear the scars.

The problematic question mark

Creativity, by definition, involves looking in new ways, a questioning of the status quo. Many churches and parachurch organisations, on the other hand, find a questioning attitude unsettling and threatening: it is too often the case that their faith is built on a foundation of conformity and answers rather than originality and questions. The classic vows of monasticism are poverty, chastity and obedience (to one's superiors), and this third injunction has been insisted upon far beyond the cloister.

I have known several young people down the years who have

undertaken gap year and other short-term mission projects with one prominent international youth outreach agency. A worryingly high number of these young people have returned home disillusioned; some have lost their faith entirely. What they found in the field were teams where tight controls on doctrine and lifestyle were rigidly enforced and any questioning of team leadership was seen as usurping spiritual authority. In many cases, the best and brightest team members, those with fresh and creative insights, were branded as troublemakers and sent home. Those who survived and thrived were the smilingly compliant. In direct and indirect ways, a message was communicated that questions were not welcome. An attitude of questioning is widely seen in many churches and Christian agencies as the antithesis of godliness. It is seen as unspiritual and rebellious.

Creativity-free church leadership

Today's church is the inheritor of a long tradition of anxiety about the artistic, the playful, the experimental and the questioning. The result is that far too many of the places where we worship have become, in the words of US missiologist Leonard Sweet, 'places of lowered expectations and diminished dreams'.[1]

Not only has the church struggled with creativity *per se*, it has struggled in particular with the idea of creative and innovative leadership. We have noted that historically the dominant model of church ministry has been that of guardian of a tradition rather than reimaginer of that tradition in changing times. We have also said that a large proportion of those who are frustrated with existing models, and are fired up to innovate, tend to do so by borrowing somebody else's blueprint. There are at least a couple of further reasons why church leadership has tended to be a creativity-free zone.

Pastoral expectations

Down the centuries, the church has rarely encouraged creative or pioneering types to see themselves as potential leaders. In part, this has been due to the main metaphor we have used for church leadership—or, rather, the way we have distorted the meaning of that metaphor.

Historically, the central image used by the church to define its leaders has been that of pastor, the Latin for 'shepherd'. 'Pastor' is one of the five key ministries needed to build up the church, as outlined by Paul in Ephesians 4:11. It draws on the biblical pattern of Jesus as shepherd (John 10; 1 Peter 2:25; Hebrews 13:20), which is based in turn on the many biblical images of God as shepherd to his people (Genesis 49:24; Psalm 23). It carries echoes of King David, who as a youth had been a shepherd and was often seen as the ideal of biblical kingship, and of Jesus' call to Peter to take care of his sheep (John 21:15–17). It is also a key image in historic accounts of church leadership, such as the Rule of St Benedict and *Pastoral Care* by Pope Gregory the Great, both from the sixth century, and Richard Baxter's 17th-century *The Reformed Pastor*.

Biblically, the role of shepherd involved the care and nurture of a group of sheep that he knew by name. It also involved moving the sheep on from familiar grazing grounds in search of new pasture, which could mean passing through dangerous terrain (Psalm 23:4), as well as going to rescue sheep that had wandered off into hazardous places (Ezekiel 34:4–5). The shepherd would be equipped with a sturdy stick that could serve as a club (Psalm 23:4), and sometimes with a sling like that of David (1 Samuel 17:40), with which to fight off wild animals and thieves. At night the shepherd would keep watch for danger, using his own body as the gateway of the sheepfold (John 10:7, 9). Secular usage of the time also used the title of shepherd to indicate strong and wise governance, and, in the writings of the prophet Isaiah, God even describes the Persian military leader Cyrus the Great as 'my shepherd' (Isaiah 44:28).

The job of shepherd required strong and resourceful people, prepared to exercise initiative, leadership, risk, rescue and confrontation, as well as commitment and nurture. So when Paul encourages the Ephesian elders to be shepherds of the church of God, the specific shepherding role he cites is that of keeping guard and being ready to fight against 'savage wolves' who would devastate the flock (Acts 20:28–29).

In recent decades, however, the church has tended to view the role of pastor through the prism of an individualistic, therapeutic culture where the search for personal identity and self-esteem has become an overriding preoccupation for adults and the main quality we hope to instil in our children.[2] The main sins in such a culture are failing to 'respect myself' and neglecting to realise my own 'unlimited potential'. I once told the story of Mary Jones and her Bible in a church primary school in south London. The heart of this remarkable story (well known to earlier generations in the UK) is of an eight-year-old Welsh girl from the late 18th century, who saved up for six years and walked barefoot for 25 miles each way to buy a Welsh Bible of her own. I asked the pupils what factors they thought motivated her extraordinary patience and endurance. The answers I received back were 'So she could feel good about herself', 'So she could respect herself', and 'To raise her self-esteem'.

In such a therapeutic culture, the pastor is expected to be on hand to help people feel happy, to help them nurture a positive self-image and discover personal fulfilment. He or she is there to help them realise their potential and manage the personal impact of life's challenges, particularly issues such as loneliness, depression and sexual and relationship issues. The pastor is not expected to be the one who critiques the values of the culture, but is expected to be the one who tends the wounds it inflicts.[3] The worship he or she leads is geared primarily towards generating warm, positive feelings towards God, rather than conveying truths about God or an unsettling challenge from God.

This distorted image of the pastor as affirming therapist, life coach and purveyor of ecstatic experiences has profoundly shaped the character of our ministry and the expectations of those who take it on. Most pastors have an inbuilt bias to nurture rather than confront. One pastorally minded colleague warned me that in her opinion, it was never right for a leader to bring about stark and wide-ranging change in a church, even if this would draw in many more people: it would cause too much pain to some members of the existing congregation. That is precisely what I was in the middle of doing, and in a sense she was right. It was a painful experience for all concerned. But the pastoral bias towards care and nurture can also entail a bias against the sort of life-saving surgery that may be urgently needed in some churches. The need for change may not be evident to members of the church in question, but all too often it is evident to outsiders.

Too many pastors in practice exercise a hospice ministry in their own church, holding the patient's hand while it dies. They may well be able to envisage creative ways forward involving change, but then a pastoral paralysis sets in. They are unwilling to wield the scalpel and risk upsetting the patient, even if the diagnosis is terminal. The result is that a choice is made by default. They in effect choose death over disharmony. This is the story not only of churches but of entire denominations.

The rest of society has happily colluded with the models of ministry offered by the churches, based on therapeutic and nurturing models. The expectations of our culture reflect the stereotypes generated by the church, but also reinforce them. One of the best and best-selling books on choosing a career is *Do What You Are* by Paul Tieger and Barbara Barron. The authors do a solid job of applying the categories of the Myers-Briggs™ personality test to the challenge of helping readers find the right job. It is noticeable, however, that the personality types with the greatest natural bias towards creativity are not guided towards 'minster of religion' as a career option, but those with a natural bias towards interpersonal warmth and empathy are.[4] The inference is clear: if you want to be creative and original, go into TV or advertising, not the church.

Leadership as science

Writings on leadership, particularly military and political leadership, have been around for centuries (including Plato in ancient Greece, Sun Tzu in ancient China and Machiavelli in Renaissance Italy). The second half of the 20th century saw the arrival of a new genre: writings on business leadership. During the 1970s, leadership studies started to be seen as a respectable subject for academic study, pioneered by the prolific scholar and business consultant Warren G. Bennis. The first doctorate in Leadership Studies opened its doors in 1979, at the University of San Diego.

So the rise of studies in business leadership took place during the era we now call modernity. This was the age that placed supreme confidence in science, progress, rationality and universal laws. Leadership, too, became understood as a science with its own laws. As recently as 1998, John Maxwell, a leadership guru in both the church and the business world, could publish a book called *The 21 Irrefutable Laws of Leadership*. The implication is clear: these are principles that have been empirically tested and their validity proven beyond all doubt. Leadership, like science, runs according to objective laws. And, for objective laws to apply, the world they describe has to be, by definition, more or less stable and predictable: it would be impossible to conceive of 'laws' in an Alice in Wonderland world where everything is unstable and constantly changing.

Trends and attitudes usually catch on in the church later than they do in the rest of society, and tend to survive there long after they have died elsewhere. This has been true of leadership theory. In recent years, students of business leadership have been noticeably more reticent about distilling 'timeless', 'scientific' and 'objective' laws for all forms of leadership, but this approach can still be found as a staple in church leadership courses and writings.

Just a year after Maxwell was writing about leadership's irrefutable laws, another book was published which questioned this entire framework. Leonard Sweet's *Aquachurch*[5] reimagines church leadership as an art rather than a science. As an art, it calls for artistic skills such as intuition, creativity and risk-taking. The book's central metaphor is that the culture of our postmodern world is fluid, unpredictable and rapidly changing. Maps of the old terrain have become redundant: today's church leader needs to master the arts of navigation. Sweet's diagnosis is unsettling but surely correct, and he opens the way for a more creative approach to church leadership.

Old attitudes die hard, though. Several generations of church leaders (all those born before the 1970s, and many since) were raised and trained in a culture where modernity set the agenda. Secular humanism was clearly the enemy and it was fought with its own weapons: the Bible was defended by evangelicals as being 'objectively true' and apologists offered forensic 'evidence that demands a verdict',[6] while liberals spoke earnestly of what 'modern man' could believe and not believe, as if that set the parameters for faith. Leaders had well-worn maps handed on by those whose ministries they admired and had seen being highly effective in their day.

It takes courage to admit that the familiar landscape has changed, that the old maps are more likely to mislead than guide. Most clergy will continue to operate according to an old paradigm with which they are comfortable, and their paradigm will eventually die with them. But during this in-between period, for much of the church, leadership is still seen as a science and its leaders still dutifully attend conferences in search of proven blueprint solutions.

A case for creativity

The anxiety so often shown by the church towards the creative arts and creative leadership is deeply ironic, given the strong Christian case to be made for human creativity.

- The first thing we know about God is that he is Creator (Genesis 1:1). Biblically, God is the wellspring of all creativity. Look around you. Go to a zoo or forest, watch any nature documentary or walk the crowded streets of any city to see the astonishing creativity of the Creator. Look up: 'The heavens declare the glory of God; the skies proclaim the work of his hands' (Psalm 19:1). Throughout the scriptures, many creative metaphors for God recur, including composer and performer, metalworker and potter, garment maker and dresser, builder and architect.[7]
- Humanity is made in the image of God (Genesis 1:26–27). The clear implication is that we are to 'image' God, at least in part, by being creative: sure enough, the first instruction God gives to humanity is the 'cultural mandate' to be creative with the raw material of the earth (vv. 28–30). It is as if God sees his creation as still unfinished and wants the cooperation of humankind to draw out its latent potential. The very first act of Adam is to think up creative names for all the animals God brings to him (2:19–20).
- The first biblical reference to the Holy Spirit being sent to empower a group of people is for a work of artistic craftsmanship. Bezalel and Oholiab are skilled in wood carving and jewellery making, as well as the design and weaving of fine garments (Exodus 35:30–35). King David danced under the influence of the same Spirit (2 Samuel 6:14), and the biblical references to music and singing are too numerous to mention. Throughout the Bible, dressing somebody in fine clothing is a sign of ennoblement; Lydia is a rep for a foreign fashion wholesaler (Acts 16:14) and Dorcas is a seamstress (9:39).

- The Old Testament prophets were given to wild dreams and visions, and many enacted dramatic visual parables, such as Jeremiah's smashing a clay jar in the municipal tip before an audience of politicians and priests (Jeremiah 19). In Ezekiel, the sign of God's blessing on a young woman (a personification of Israel) is that he gives her fine embroidered clothes, jewellery and a nose-ring (Ezekiel 16:10–13).
- A key biblical vision of eternity is of a vibrant centre of commerce and culture, a city into which the rulers of the earth bring all the richest and most creative aspects of human culture, even pagan cultures (Isaiah 60).[8]
- The prophet Joel foresees a day when God will pour out his Spirit on all people, a day that will bring in an era of dreams and visions (Joel 2:28). Peter quotes Joel's vision on the day of Pentecost, proclaiming that this Spirit-inspired era of wonder and imagination has begun (Acts 2:14–21).
- Jesus was trained from childhood as a carpenter and general builder, and may well have worked with his father on the Roman new town of Sepphoris, just three miles from Nazareth. His later teaching ministry reveals him to be a master of metaphor, epigram, hyperbole and humour, not to mention a compelling storyteller. One of the people Jesus commends most strongly is the woman who recklessly pours out a jar of eye-wateringly expensive perfume (worth an entire year's wages) over his feet (Mark 14:3–9). Jesus loves this dramatic symbolic gesture.
- The apostle Paul is clearly well versed in the Greek-speaking culture and arts of his day. He is fond of quoting from Greek poets (see Acts 17:22–31, where he quotes from several of them, and Titus 1:12, where he quotes Epimenides of Crete). Likewise, Paul regularly draws analogies from music, philosophy and sport. The New Testament as a whole contains more than 100 examples of quotations, borrowings or adaptations from ancient authors such as Aeschylus, Sophocles, Plutarch, Tacitus, Xenophon, Aristotle and Seneca.[9]

- The Bible contains a wide diversity of literary styles, including love poetry, proverb, narrative, history, apocalypse, elegy, epic, romance, tragedy, satire and narrative, not to mention literary techniques such as puns and acrostics (needless to say, some of these techniques are not immediately obvious to the majority of us who read the Bible in translation). The Bible's content ranges from ecstatic visions to expressions of grief and blank depression, via wry humour and blatant eroticism. Not only does the Bible point towards creativity, but it is creative in its very form.

There is an overwhelming Christian case for creativity and imagination,[10] and when we put our minds to it, we do rather well: think of the intricate artwork of The Book of Kells, the music of J.S. Bach, the poems of Milton, Gerard Manley Hopkins and T.S. Eliot, the cathedrals and stained glass of medieval Europe, the children's stories of C.S. Lewis, the paintings of Rembrandt and the novels of Dostoyevsky, for starters. Creativity should be the default setting for Christians in general and church leaders in particular. Hold on to that idea while we digress for a few moments.

A case for creative leadership

Leonard Sweet is right. We live in an age where many of the familiar landmarks are being washed away, an era of unparalleled cultural change. Erwin McManus, leader of the pioneering Mosaic church in Los Angeles, is right to see our time of rapid change as an extraordinary window of opportunity for the church to rethink at a fundamental level how we live, worship and communicate. For McManus, the disorientation of our era presents Christians with an opportunity, not a problem: 'Those of us who live in this window of history must consider ourselves uniquely appointed by God.'[11]

The kinds of new social, cultural, environmental and religious challenges we face in Western culture should by now be familiar to most readers. These include the shift from a modern to a postmodern way of thinking, with its suspicion of truth-claims and absolutes, plus a slippery tendency to hold on to incompatible truths at the same time. This is combined with new ways of making sense of identity—the self as a project constantly to be reinvented, particularly through dress and other patterns of consumption.

Then there is the acceleration of communications technologies, including the internet, with its exciting possibilities and new demons, such as online addictions and 'information anxiety' caused by having too much data at our fingertips. There is a dramatic rise in mobility, within nations and across borders, plus a large shift globally from rural areas to the cities (for the first time in history, more people now live in cities than on the land). In most parts of the world, this has resulted in increasingly diverse populations in increasingly large urban centres, and an unprecedented rise in levels of loneliness and depression. Interestingly, at the same time as the UK's cities have been growing, there has been an even larger migration to our rural areas: around 80,000 British people move from towns and cities to the countryside each year, many in search of a greater sense of community and belonging.[12]

In global economic terms, the picture is a mixed one. The good news is that the number of people living on less than a dollar a day has almost halved in the two decades spanning the late 20th and early 21st centuries, due mainly to economic reforms in India and China; the proportion of undernourished people in the world has almost halved in the past 50 years, and the mortality rate for children has more than halved during the same period.[13] The bad news is that the very poorest billion people in our world continue to become poorer,[14] and there is increasing inequality within affluent societies, as well as globally. (In 2000, UK company CEOs were paid 47 times average pay; by 2010 this had risen to 81 times average.)[15]

We face a population explosion. At the time of writing, the world's population stood at around 6.9 billion (from 6 billion back in 1999). By 2050 it is projected to reach almost 9 billion. This, combined with the rapid growth of affluence and aspiration around the globe, is putting unprecedented pressures on the natural resources of the planet, leading to growing dangers from climate change, with associated questions about our relationship to the environment and our legacy for future generations.

At the same time, we see a new openness in the West to spirituality and mysticism, combined with a widespread mistrust of established religion;[16] an explosion in religious faith globally, especially in China and Africa, and particularly towards Pentecostalism and Islam.[17] There is a shift towards fundamentalism within religions, which brings social consequences (most notably in relation to terrorism and the role of women), combined with a catastrophic decline in church membership in the UK and Western Europe, particularly among children and young people (only four per cent of British children now attend church). The number of pastors leaving the ministry is high (ordained clergy leaving the Church of England each year average around 220,[18] while a 1998 Focus on the Family survey estimated the rate in the USA across all denominations as 1500 a month, due to burn-out, conflict within the church and moral failure). A growing number of churchgoers are disillusioned with their own tradition (with a consequent rise in those identi-fying with labels such as post-evangelical, post-liberal and post-charismatic), and there is a widespread sense among many church leaders that the old ways of doing things just don't work any longer.

It is not simply that we are in a culture of rapid change. We are in a culture of rapid, discontinuous change, the sort of change that takes place when a culture is undergoing a major upheaval.[19] Most cultural change for most of human history has been continuous, which means that it is slower, more predictable and grows naturally out of current conditions. In such societies, established solutions work well or require only minor modifications. The young have reason to value the wisdom of older people because the experience the elders have accumulated remains applicable.

Discontinuous change means that the pace of change itself is accelerating so fast that the old world is barely recognisable. Conventional theories and ways of operating seem not to work any longer. The old are more likely to ask the young to help them navigate the changing times, rather than vice versa. It is a time of cultural disorientation and anxiety. In such a time, the challenge to the church is simple and compelling: changing times need a changing approach to leadership. The church urgently needs a new generation of leaders who are navigators (Sweet), cultural architects (McManus), and pioneer ministers (Fresh Expressions). It needs leaders who are agents of change rather than opponents of change. Our churches should be places that engage the culture rather than stand as a refuge from it and complain about it.

This is all undeniably true. In practice, though, faced with unprecedented and accelerating change all around them, and plagued by a growing sense that the world in which they were trained to minister no longer exists, most church leaders carry on doing what they have always done, but with diminishing returns and greater depression and burn-out.

There is, however, another reason why we need to be creative leaders, fired up to shape unique and creative churches, and this reason goes beyond pure pragmatism. It is because creativity ought to be second nature to us. We are made in the image of a creative God, who calls us to creativity; we worship a Lord who embodies creativity; we are empowered by the Spirit who energises creativity; we are guided by scriptures that model creativity. Leaders are called to be creative because of who God is and who we are meant to be.

If we see creativity as essentially a pragmatic response to declining numbers or an era of intense cultural change, we risk missing the point. This viewpoint implies that the church has no mandate for creativity in the quiet, stable eras of history. It also risks lulling the church into a false sense of security—as if, once we have got to grips with the new era, we can relax back into familiar patterns and predictability, a reassuring new status quo. But our calling is to be more than pragmatists: it is to be artists, poets, dreamers and out-of-the-box thinkers. It is to be explorers who make new roads and rediscover old roads.

Then again, this is not just an issue of church leadership. Our approach to leadership says something deeper about our way of looking at the world and what it means to be human, as well as what it means to be a believer. Am I somebody who looks around and sees life as a series of problems requiring brisk and effective solutions? Or do I glimpse an intriguing path along which I long to journey with others, never quite knowing what I might find? Do I aspire to being a CEO or a pilgrim?

The late Donald Allchin, an Anglican scholar and author, over time became increasingly interested in the spirituality of Wales, especially its spiritual poetry. Allchin wrote:

To know the world as the poet, or as the person who prays, knows it is to know it primarily as a mystery which is not closed but open to us and which summons us to ever deeper knowledge and understanding. In this perspective the world itself and every place within the world is seen not as a problem to be mastered and explained away but a reality greater than ourselves to be progressively explored and known, loved and praised.[20]

Self-evidently, this approach will not result in a model of church leadership that is fast and convenient, predictable and risk-free. Quite the opposite: the model will be slow and inconvenient, unpredictable and risky. It involves heading out on a journey into the unknown. It is an adventure.

The travel writer Paul Theroux once mused in *The Washington Post* that 'travel is only glamorous in retrospect'. He is right: it is only as we look back on a successful journey that we can savour and idealise it. The same applies to the journey of shaping a unique and creative church. Perhaps one day, as we approach the end of the journey, we will be able to look back and see some kind of logic and direction to the path we have helped to make. For now, we shall regularly make mistakes and may get lost from time to time; we shall spend a surprising amount of our time improvising. But that is OK, because that is the stuff of adventures.

What this adventure might look like in practice will be the subject of the rest of this book.

Snapshot: Urban arts

The roots of Grace Church, Hackney, lie in London's most high-profile conservative evangelical church, St Helen's Bishopsgate. But although it is only a short walk away from St Helen's, and shares the Reformed theology of its parent church, in other respects Grace Church is a world away. Many people meeting Grace these days would struggle to recognise her as the daughter of Helen.

It all began when a curate of St Helen's, Andrew Jones, had a vision for planting a church among the arts community of Hackney in East London. Discussions with London Diocese opened up the option of a church plant into the prominent setting of St Leonard's, Shoreditch, in the Deanery of Hackney and close to a significant portion of East London's arts community. St Leonard's, best known as the setting of the BBC sitcom Rev, had no evening service of its own and was happy to welcome the newcomers.

From the start, Grace Church aspired to connect with the local arts world and deliberately chose to model an ethos and style quite different from the more traditional conservative evangelical style of St Helen's, with its focus on the spoken word and relative lack of emphasis on the visual arts.

Andrew and the leadership of Grace Church work hard to make their services aesthetic events where creative types will feel at home. A recent Advent service opened with a traditional Eastern Orthodox call to worship called *toaca*, which involves a person hammering a long piece of wood rhythmically with a wooden hammer. This led into singing a number of old Advent hymns, to the accompaniment of instruments including a piano accordion, steel guitar and viola. During Communion, a folk singer sang a version of 'Glory bound' by Canadian folk trio The Wailin' Jennys.

Music in other services has included Mozart, Bach, Messiaen, John Cage, Philip Glass and the country-roots of Gillian Welch. The evening I attended a service, we received the bread and wine of Communion to the accompaniment of avant-garde opera.

The Grace Church community watches films together and Andrew lectures in a local bar on themes from film that interact with the Christian faith. The community hosts a fiction reading group and gives local artists the opportunity to display their work. Recently a member of the church studying at the Slade School of Art presented a sound installation after a service.

Andrew notes that Grace Church deliberately blends the ancient and modern, the formal and the informal in worship, flowing from the community's theological convictions, which he describes as 'Reformed and Catholic' (in other words, rooted in the Reformation but keen to maintain continuity with the church that went before). He says that many creative people appreciate the beauty and form of the liturgies used in services. The church shares the Lord's Supper every week, as they see it as a verbal and enacted proclamation of Christ's death. Andrew adds that it is a gift of God to embrace all human senses, and that people are not just ears! Intriguingly, he says that they try to make the journey to the Communion table as chaotic as possible: they actively want people to experience a degree of disorientation as opposed to the predictability found in some churches; they 'want people to bump into each other'.

Grace Church Hackney aims to model inclusiveness: it works on the assumption that many of those present will not be Christians and that some will even be hostile to the faith. The church aims never to stereotype or mock the beliefs of others, and most services are followed by an opportunity for open discussion. Andrew Jones says that they aim for services that do not come across as 'slick and cheesy'.

4

Unique church

Slow food

In 1986 McDonalds was drawing up plans to open a fast-food outlet close to the historic Spanish Steps in Rome. A group of campaigners banded together to block the move, under the leadership of local resident Carlo Petrini. Petrini felt that important wider issues were at stake and was concerned that his campaign should be wider than simply blocking the arrival of American fast-food restaurants. He wanted to make a positive statement about key values underlying the sale, production, culture and consumption of all food.

In particular, he wanted to help preserve traditional regional cuisines, along with the lore that often surrounds them, and to support local food and wine producers. He also wanted to encourage the kind of leisurely social dining among wider families and friends that was characteristic of traditional Mediterranean culture but was under threat from the trend towards rapid and solitary 'grazing'. And he was passionate about encouraging authentic home cooking in the face of the quick-and-easy convenience foods marketed by the supermarkets. As a deliberate response to the concept and culture of fast food, he named the new movement Slow Food.

Slow church

In its rejection of imported, mass-produced, quick, one-size-fits-all models, the Slow Food movement could serve as an inspiration for creative church leaders looking to shape unique and creative churches. We could call them Slow Churches. (Contrast Bill Hybels' description of his Willow Creek megachurch near Chicago as a 'high-speed, high-intensity organisation', which employs the sort of staff who drive mostly in the fast lane. Hybels explicitly commends the busy CEO of a large corporation who interrupts the waiter in a European-style restaurant in the US with an abrupt 'Would you please go into the kitchen and bring out whatever is hot so we can eat right away? I don't care what you bring as long as you can bring it fast.')[1]

Carlo Petrini's vital insight is that speed is not always a virtue and that locality matters. In an age of growing globalisation and homogenisation, Slow Food is about celebrating the specific and the distinctive: the *appellation contrôlée* wine, the local cheese, the vegetables currently in season from local producers.

This should not come as a new idea to those strands of the Christian tradition with a strong tradition of place, such as the traditional Anglican parish system and the Catholic church with its emphasis on local festivities and pilgrimage. The Reformed tradition, from Luther and Calvin onward, has been more ambivalent about a spirituality rooted in a particular location, partly as a reaction against what it saw as the superstitious cults of local saints and the threat of nature-based paganism. Protestant and evangelical churches have typically taught that there are no 'holy places' and have identified the 'true' church as being an eclectic body of the elect known only to God. The evangelical witness to the encounter with God is usually to a Jesus located 'in my heart'; the central motif of evangelical theology has been redemption rather than incarnation. Evangelicals have generally had little time for the sacramental (the idea that the central place where we encounter God is through material channels such as water, bread and wine). Many pastors routinely teach that the sacraments are nothing in themselves: all that matters is the inner faith that accompanies them.

Little surprise, then, that evangelicals have tended to show little interest in a spirituality of place, have often been cheerleaders for the abolition of the parish system, have felt relaxed about the principle of eclectic churches to which the faithful travel over great distances, have typically felt little responsibility for the community in which their building happens to be located, and have tended to see secular material culture as a distraction from faith rather than the place where God is to be found.

This evangelical emphasis has been misleading and unhelpful, even if many of its anxieties are sincerely motivated. It is misleading because there is no spirituality without place, no spirituality that is not embodied and specific. Jesus of Nazareth was born to a particular woman, in a particular stable, in a particular village, in a particular region of the Roman Empire. The Gospel writers are at pains to emphasise the specificity of it all, even down to the names of the people who were Roman emperor and governor of Syria at the time (Luke 2:1–2). The Gospels and epistles are written with specific audiences in mind, in specific places, as are the letters to the seven churches of Revelation with their mass of detailed local cultural and historical references.

It is true that, from earliest times, the Church understood the biblical principle that the dwelling-place of God is no longer a temple, but people. The human body is now the temple of the Spirit, both individually (1 Corinthians 6:19) and corporately (Ephesians 2:21–22). So the focus of Christianity has rightly been more about the holiness of people than the holiness of places. But to ignore the spirituality of place is to ignore the fact that all the people and congregations in whom the Spirit resides are embodied. We encounter God not by somehow rising above the material details of life or stepping outside time, but remaining inside them.

Just as the Jerusalem temple had been the physical location where God's presence was encountered, so now, says Paul (in the above references), God's temple in Corinth and Ephesus is the believers who live in those cities. There can be no encounter with God except through bodies, cultures and places. Today, too, the work of the Spirit always has a Global Positioning System (GPS) reference.

Even the Reformers understood this principle, despite their suspicion of holy places. Martin Luther relocated the ideal setting for living out the Christian faith away from the monastery and into the busy world of home, family and work. Calvin recognised that the earth is a 'theatre of glory' where we daily encounter the glory of God.

This is entirely biblical. Matthew underlines the incarnational principle that Jesus came as Immanuel, God with us, at a specific place and time and in a specific culture (Matthew 1:23). His birth was no pure, sanitised event, in the perfect 'holy' culture so characteristic of the world of religious myths. It was preceded by a futile and depressing attempt to find suitable lodgings and was followed by a visit from the local shepherds. Despite the positive image of the shepherd in scripture, shepherds were at the bottom of the heap in terms of social status. They would often look after other people's flocks and had a reputation for stealing newborn lambs or kids. This happened so often that rabbis advised people never to buy wool or goat's milk directly from shepherds because they would probably be buying stolen goods. Shepherds were not allowed to testify in court because their word was not considered trustworthy. Yet these were the first witnesses of the incarnation.

Jesus said that the place we are most likely to meet him is in the people we encounter in our everyday lives, particularly those who are suffering or in trouble (Matthew 25:31–46). We are each called by God to live out our faith in a particular place, with a particular group of people, at a particular moment in history. This is where we both encounter God and form our own identity, and that makes the context of our life and ministry holy ground.

Eight-way attentiveness

Shaping a unique and creative church is not about bolting on novelties and gimmicks in worship, or introducing change for the sake of change. Nor is it about panting after our rapidly shifting culture as it races round the next bend. New wine requires new wineskins (Luke 5:37–39), but the wine should always be *appellation contrôlée*, with the name of a local vineyard and the year of production clearly stamped on the label.

This sounds fine in theory, but it runs counter to most of the church growth initiatives of the 20th century, which tended to suggest that a successful model from one setting can easily be transplanted to another. A noticeable shift in emphasis began with the *Mission-Shaped Church* report of 2004. This suggested that church planters in particular need to practise a 'double listening': to the surrounding culture and to what the report calls 'the inherited tradition of the gospel and the church'.[2]

In fact, this process of careful listening to a local context applies not only to church planters but to all who wish to influence the shape of any local church, of whatever tradition. At the same time, I would suggest that the two broad terms 'culture' and 'inherited tradition of the gospel and the church' are rather too general to be useful. They roll together too many disparate ideas, so key points risk being missed. I would suggest that a more helpful way forward involves unravelling the various aspects of culture and church to which a local leader needs to be attentive. I have become convinced that creative leadership of a unique church centres on an eight-way attentiveness.

To separate out as many as eight areas might sound daunting and over-complex. In reality, though, this kind of multiple attentiveness is what many of us in church leadership practise automatically, day in, day out, but without labelling it as such. The following eight forms of attentiveness are simply an attempt to unravel and examine the strands of what many effective local ministers do instinctively.

The eight strands are:

1 The local community
2 The local church
3 People's unique stories
4 Events
5 The biblical story
6 Our historic roots
7 An inherited tradition
8 Where the Spirit is at work

The local community

One of my favourite news stories of recent years comes from South Africa. Some game wardens were transporting a leopard from one safari park to another in a van. The van was involved in a traffic accident, whereupon its back doors burst open and the leopard escaped into the suburbs of Johannesburg. The game wardens called in a team of trained hunters to trap the leopard so that nobody would get hurt and they would not have to shoulder the blame for losing the animal. The hunters duly arrived and started searching the suburbs of Johannesburg. They carried out a detailed exploration of public parks and residential streets, around public buildings and in private gardens.

On their very first night of searching, the trained hunters found no fewer than seven leopards, all located in the suburbs of the city. It was only when people started looking for a leopard that they found there had been several of them there all along, wild and wonderful, hidden in the residential suburbs. Most of us little suspect how many leopards may be hiding in our own neighbourhoods!

The least explored place on earth is the world on my own doorstep, because it is the one place I most take for granted. But this is the world to which I am called to minister. An essential component of local church ministry involves getting to know my own patch intimately. It involves asking questions such as:

- What kind of area do we live in (rural, urban, suburban…), and how does this affect our model of what it is to be church? A rural church is more likely to see itself as serving the whole parish and to value inclusiveness, whereas an urban or suburban church is more likely to operate on a 'competitive and consumerist' model, offering something distinctive in the marketplace of church styles.[3]
- What is the history of our local area?
- Does recent local history show continuity or radical discontinuity with the past?
- Precisely who is out there (in terms of ethnic background, class, regional backgrounds, employment patterns, attitudes to faith in general and to our church in particular)? Is ours a very diverse area or fairly homogeneous? If it is diverse, do the different groups relate to each other or stay apart? Are there strong kinship networks locally, and how does this affect the dynamic of the area?
- Is ours primarily a residential area, a business district, a farming community, or something else? How does that affect the kind of people who are around, and at what time of day? For example, do many people leave the area for work during the day or come into it? Are the only people at home during the day young parents with babies and toddlers?

In part, this kind of information can be found in formal ways:

- Using census data, easily accessible via the website of the UK's Office of National Statistics (www.neighbourhood.statistics.gov.uk), and information on wealth and poverty, which can be found in the *Index of Multiple Deprivation*.
- Conducting a parish audit.[4]
- Reading local newspapers, and spending time in a local library.
- Consulting local history societies, residents' groups and action groups.

The aim is to build up as clear a picture as possible of the recent history of the area, who is out there and the kind of lives they lead. In my Strawberry Hill parish, for example, the 2001 census showed that 93.6 per cent of local residents were white. Two-thirds were under the age of 45, with almost all the remainder being under 60. Half the population had the very highest levels of academic and professional qualifications (levels 4 and 5), with fewer than ten per cent of people having no formal qualifications. In terms of economic classification, the majority fell into the category of 'Lower Managerial and Professional', followed by 'Higher Professional' and 'Higher Managerial'. In other words, this was posh, white, young, affluent suburbia—and those facts would inevitably have to shape the ministry of the church in that area.

We then moved to Kennington in inner-city south London. Again, the parish was predominantly young (fully 78 per cent being under the age of 45), but with a very different ethnic mix and economic profile, including a large West African community and significant numbers of professionals in their 20s and working in their first jobs in London. Almost a quarter of local residents had no qualifications at all. The area was home to a number of teenage street gangs, as well as a number of Members of Parliament, since the parish is just across the river from Westminster. We were also next door to the 'Vauxhall gay village', which by some estimates constituted as many as 20 per cent of people in the local area and attracted vast numbers of visitors. Again, the make-up of the area had to shape the character of the ministry. It would evidently be impossible to exercise the same sort of ministry in Kennington as I had exercised in Twickenham. The leader's first task is to listen to the community.

Census and other statistical data are a vital tool for the church leader, but there is no substitute for simply walking the streets of an area and getting to know the local people—chatting with them in the parks and shops, in coffee shops and in the pub, at the school gate, over a meal, in the gym, or walking the dog. There is no substitute for hearing about people's hopes, dreams and anxieties first-hand.

A priority for any church leader should be to ensure that their working week is not so dominated by resourcing Christians and church activities that they neglect making time to loiter with intent and meet non-church people, who make up the majority of people in our locality, in non-church settings. In Twickenham this did not take much effort, since we had a long stream of unchurched people beating a path to our door and inviting me to their homes, largely due to baptism requests and because church attendance was an admission criterion for our church school. In Kennington it took greater effort, since the workload of church meetings and expectations from congregation members were greater and there were fewer baptisms. The simple fact is that any leader who aspires to a missional encounter with his or her local community has to spend a significant amount of time getting to know that community and its people.

This is what cross-cultural missionaries have been doing for centuries: analysing the local culture; learning the language and customs in order to be able to communicate with the people. Until relatively recently, the church in the West assumed that the hard work of contextualised mission was not needed for our own culture: people here were already sufficiently familiar with the Christian story. It was assumed that the role of the church in Western culture was essentially pastoral rather than missionary, acting as a chaplain to the faithful. We even had different words for outreach abroad and at home: 'mission' and 'evangelism'. Within a generation, however, the world has changed. The once 'Christian' nation of Great Britain has become a nation where less than eight per cent of the population is in church on a Sunday (a far lower figure in some parts of the country and across some sectors of society), and, of the remaining 92 per cent, most have little knowledge of Christianity and even less interest in it.[5]

In Chapter 1 we recalled the experience of the British missionary bishop Lesslie Newbigin, who returned home from India in 1974, only to find that Britain itself had become a post-Christian culture. In his seminal 1986 book, *Foolishness to the Greeks: The Gospel and Western Culture*, he calls for a missionary encounter with his own culture. For a number of years in the late 1980s and early 1990s, I used to visit Lesslie Newbigin at home in his retirement, and this was a theme to which he returned on many occasions. For some of this time, I was writing my book of Christian perspectives on fashion and image. It was encouraging, if slightly unexpected, to find this venerable missionary bishop keen to discuss the cultural meanings of punk haircuts and designer labels. Newbigin's ground-breaking agenda should, by now, be mainstream. Basic skills of contextualisation, as required by cross-cultural missionaries, should now be imperative for any local church.

It is also helpful to keep an eye on shifts and patterns in the wider culture, in so far as these have an impact on what goes on locally. No local culture exists in a vacuum, especially in these days of the internet and globalised commerce and media. Relevant cultural trends might include economic changes, patterns of migration of people, and shifts in values and morality (such as a dramatic shift in popular attitudes towards cohabitation and gay lifestyle within a single generation). People in our own community will also be influenced by broader shifts in the way our society approaches truth and meaning ('There's no such thing as absolute truth'; 'I have my truth, you have yours'). Changes in the way people think and live have been accelerated by the arrival of the internet, presenting as it does a vast range of opinions, from the wise to the loopy, as if they were all equally valid or plausible.

Some might question our focus on locality, pointing out that a local community has a decreasing significance for most people, compared with virtual online networks and networks of personally constructed identities (based on fashion, sexuality, music and so on). They could also point out that our increasing mobility has led to people putting down shallower roots in a local community. This is a particular thrust of the *Mission-Shaped Church* report, which rightly notes the increasing importance of networks in the lives of people today.[6] This in turn has given rise to many churches based more on relational networks than on locality.

Some people have been over-hasty, though, in sounding the death knell for churches serving a local community. The reality is that the diminishing role of place in people's lives has left an aching gap. People may find that they have 200 or more 'friends' on Facebook but they do not know their next-door neighbour, and, when it comes down to it, they have nobody to go to the cinema or share a drink with on a Friday evening. A report from the UK's Mental Health Foundation in 2010, *The Lonely Society*, found that loneliness is reaching epidemic proportions, particularly among the young. The report noted that the proportion of people living alone, male and female, doubled between 1972 and 2008. Living alone does not by itself, of course, automatically equate to loneliness. Many people are content to live alone, and some sense a vocation to the solitary life. In practice, however, the numbers living alone have undoubtedly contributed to a corresponding rise in loneliness. Nearly 60 per cent of those aged 18–34 questioned in the *Lonely Society* report admitted to feeling lonely.

While technology has been wildly successful in creating vast networks of online friendships, there is clear evidence that it is being used as a substitute for real human interaction. This became clear to me during our time in Twickenham. The longing for authentic relationships in that suburban west London community created an extraordinary opportunity for the local church. More than ever, people were wanting a real place to call home, a place where others knew their name and smiled at them in the street. I would estimate that more than three-quarters of all the families I visited cited a desire to find community as their major reason for reconnecting with church. In our urban and suburban areas, the church has a unique opportunity to create an alternative community, where other forms of community are practically non-existent. Rural areas, on the other hand, tend to be naturally stronger in what sociologists term 'social capital'. The smaller numbers of people who live in a village or market town make anonymity and loneliness less likely than in the city, so there is usually less need for the church to create community from scratch. But in rural areas, too, the church has an important role in valuing and encouraging members' involvement in the wider community.

One thing is certain. In urban, suburban and rural settings alike, the rise of the eclectic church model, where people may travel over great distances to worship, has not helped. It makes church into little more than another virtual experience with people who look and sound rather like myself. Church becomes yet another consumer choice that I make. This in turn diminishes my exposure to people I find less than conducive, and reduces the risk of challenge to my lifestyle and attitudes. Interestingly, Jesus defines our neighbours not as those people who are like ourselves, but as random people in our community, different from ourselves, thrown our way by events, who give us an opportunity to show generosity and kindness (Luke 10:25–37).

Eugene Peterson's advice on looking for the right church sounds, in some ways, rather old fashioned: the smaller and nearer the better.[7] But it points to a much-needed rediscovery of place and belonging for a lonely and alienated society.

The American poet Robert Frost reflected in a 1916 interview that 'You can't be universal without being provincial'. In his case, that meant a focus on the rural life of New England and its colloquial forms of language. In Christian terms, it means that we access the universal majesty and purposes of God not by somehow lifting ourselves above the particularities of place and time, but by paying close attention to those details. The specific and local is where we find the God of eternity. In other words, the leader of the unique church needs to be attentive to his or her unique local setting, because it is holy ground.

The local church

It can be tempting for church leaders to carry in their mind an idealised vision of what their church ought to be like—based, perhaps, on a combination of the book of Acts, biblical images (body and bride of Christ, army, temple, household of God and so on) and thriving churches they know. The inevitable consequence is that, in time, the leader becomes all too aware of the yawning gap between the glorious ideal and the often grim reality in front of them: the half-heartedness and lack of commitment, the personal dysfunctions, the gossip and carping.

The reality is that no church leader starts with an ideal congregation or a blank sheet of paper. To change the metaphor, we build with the bricks we have, not those we don't have. It is essential that leaders are attentive to their own church, its history, gifts, weaknesses and opportunities, rather than wishing away the building materials with which they have been entrusted and looking longingly over the fence at a neighbour's bricks.

Attentiveness to the local church will include sensitivity to areas such as:

- The story of our church. When was it founded? What was the need or vision that caused it to be founded?
- The churchmanship tradition. Evangelical? Liberal? Catholic? Broad church? Charismatic? A mixture? Where is the existing congregation in relation to that tradition? Keen to uphold it? Open to insights from other traditions? Are there tensions in the congregation over this issue?
- The size of the church. Is it large, or tiny?
- The story of this church in recent years. Has there been a slow, gradual evolution with the usual ups and downs? A looking back to a golden age in the past? Or a disruptive trauma?[8]
- The ethnic and social mix. Does the church reflect the mix of the local community? How does this mix affect people's expectations and the type of ministry we offer?

- The 'body language' of the building. Is it austere? Informal? Historic? Contemporary?
- Other churches in the area. This will inevitably have an impact on the ministry of our church. Do we have a megachurch down the road that vacuums up lively Christians for miles around? Are we offering something similar to the other local churches, or something distinctive? Are we the only church in our area?
- The most influential members or groups within the church. Who are they?
- The kind of ministry exercised by our predecessors here. Are there aspects of this that I can learn from and build on, or are there aspects that need to be undone as quickly as possible?
- Public community buildings in the area. Is our church the only one, or one among many?
- Local perceptions of the church. Are we seen locally as having 'fuzzy' boundaries and being welcoming to newcomers, or as aloof and unwelcoming?
- The distinctive opportunities and limitations that we start with, as we try to connect with local people.

All of these factors, and more, will invariably shape our ministry. At the risk of repeating the obvious, we start where we are; we build with the bricks we have.

This became particularly clear to me during my years in Twickenham. My central calling at Holy Trinity was to help revitalise a flagging congregation. On the other side of Twickenham was one of the largest and liveliest Anglican churches in the country. If I had secretly hoped that some of their active members who lived nearby might defect and support the exciting new ministry down the road, I soon realised my mistake. It takes a lot to make people change church, especially if it means giving up the range of ministries on offer in a larger church. Furthermore, a 'graft' of members from that church to ours was never an option, as it was already planting a number of daughter churches of its own.

All the books I consulted and most other leaders I spoke to insisted that the only way to grow a church was to gather a team of passionate believers with a love of scripture and a vision for mission, make them into the church's new inner core, get them into a network of home-groups and work with them to carry out evangelistic events locally. We never did develop that sort of evangelistic inner core, and we never did succeed in sustaining a single home-group for long (most of our members were young families, with one or both adults arriving home late from work in central London). Importing a team from another church was not an option, and waiting for such people to move into the parish never worked either, partly because when this type of Christian moved into the area, they usually made a beeline for the larger church down the road. Who could blame them? It was a good church.

So church growth had to start with what we had, rather than what we didn't have—and, as it turned out, what we had was something that professional young families in the area wanted. There were three things, in fact: links to a good church primary school, baptism services, and a church hall that could provide a high-profile venue for clubs and events. These were to form the basis of our mission.

As with many church schools, our link primary school set an admissions policy that named regular attendance at our church for a year as a criterion for priority admission, so we had a regular flow of passing traffic from families who may not have had the slightest interest in faith but were keen to get a child into the school. In many ways (even as I watched the streams of newcomers pouring in through our doors), I resented this, as it felt as if the church was being 'used' by pushy parents. But there was no doubting that it gave us an extraordinary opportunity to connect with families who would not have been in church otherwise.

Similarly, this was a parish where large numbers of families wanted baptism for their children. With around 50 baptisms a year, many of my evenings were spent on baptism visits. Again, my temptation was to be cynical: we were simply being 'used' by families who would never be seen again. Still, there was no doubting the mission opportunity that it presented. We stipulated that families had to be attending Sunday worship for several months before I would talk to them about baptism, a condition with which they happily complied. During these months, a few cobwebs were blown off their mental stereotypes of church and many of them realised that they actually rather liked it.

Thirdly, we had a room attached to our church which was an ideal size for hire to local dance and drama groups, clubs and children's parties. When I first arrived, this room was piled with mountains of junk and was unusable either by the church or the community. Over a period of time, we cleared it and carried out a major refurbishment of the room. Eventually the space was being used for nearly 50 hours a week by community groups, and bringing in more than £20,000 for the church each year. More importantly, it brought in hundreds of local families each week to the church premises and gave us an opportunity to meet them and introduce them to the ministries of our church.

The demographics of the area and what we had to offer as a church came together in a remarkable way. Our mission strategy ended up being based entirely on drawing in young families who had little, if any, church background—through the link with the school, baptism requests and hire of the hall. These factors drew them in, but the other side of the same coin, and the harder part, was keeping them.

In order to retain the newcomers, we deliberately prioritised two areas. One was making Sunday worship accessible to outsiders. Partly, this involved asking our 'fringe' what they really found helpful in worship (rather than deciding what we thought they ought to want, or what we wanted ourselves) and making tangible changes to what we did in the light of their comments. The result was a fairly traditional but accessible service with lots of traditional hymns, a thoughtful sermon related to real-life issues and a major focus on children's work. As we had a low proportion of members who were mature in faith, we had to take the risk of appointing some relative newcomers to lead children's groups, trusting that (as proved to be the case) the adults would learn and grow spiritually at the same time as the children. The alternative would have been no children's groups at all. Some would have considered this a risky option, but in practice it worked well.

The other area we prioritised was creating a sense of community. This emerged as a clear theme from my baptism visits: as already mentioned, the young families who made up the majority of the parish craved a deeper sense of belonging, which provided a unique opportunity for a church located at the heart of their community. We welcomed people unconditionally and made it clear that they were very welcome to be fellow travellers with us, whatever their faith or lack of it. This combination of accessible services and an unconditional sense of belonging gave us an unusually high retention rate of school and baptism families.

Some of the old congregation left as the church they had known and loved began to change. Many more joined. By the time I left for a new job, nine years later, Sunday attendance had grown from around 30 to around 250, and most of these people were either new to church or returning to church after many years. The influx of new members included a high proportion of sceptics and atheists. Some of our best evangelists were the atheists, who loved being a part of our church community, appreciated the facilities and groups we offered for their children and liked to engage with the sermons.

I tell this story not to trumpet my own skill as a strategic leader. Quite the opposite. I never fully shook off the temptation to envy the megachurch down the road. Even as dozens of newcomers were pouring into our Sunday services, I daydreamed about how wonderful it would be to have the staff, resources and prayer groups of the larger church. I also found it hard to shake off a sense that the 'proper' way to grow a church was to do what all the books said: have a spiritually fired-up core team to arrange passionate prayer vigils, join home-groups and take a lead in tried-and-tested evangelistic activities. For a time in the mid-2000s, our church grew at an astonishingly rapid rate, but I am ashamed to admit that I spent much of that period feeling resentful about the newcomers' motives for attending, unsettled that we attracted atheists rather than keen Christians (what was so wrong with our services that Christians weren't interested?), and secretly envious of other people's ministries. If Freud had studied such things, he might have diagnosed a case of parish envy.

Looking back, it is hard to believe I was so lacking in insight and appreciation. My only comfort is that Jesus' own disciples were not much better at seeing when God was doing something new and creative in their midst. As Jesus said to the couple who were walking alongside him on the road to Emmaus, but spectacularly failing to recognise him, 'How foolish you are, and how slow to believe...!' (Luke 24:25). The lesson from this era in my ministry was a simple one, but one to which I seemed curiously resistant. I had to value the bricks I had rather than the bricks I didn't have. The very resources and opportunities that our church needed to engage our local community were already there.

The church leader needs some basic skills in analysing the history and identity of a local congregation. Part of this process might involve finding metaphors or analogies to describe what is going on. In one of my churches I thought in terms of agricultural seasons: I recognised that my job was to break up stony ground, till the soil and prepare it for seeds, and that would not happen quickly. This slow, painful work would be vital preparation for a rich harvest one day, but it was unlikely to happen in my time. The analogy helped give me patience and perspective when my daily work felt mostly like a disillusioning and unproductive grind.

For another of my churches, the best analogy I could find was the plot of a novel: Golding's *Lord of the Flies*, in which a group of schoolboys descend into anarchy on a desert island. It seemed to me that this particular church was not so much a coherent community as a leaderless group of individuals doing their own thing, often hurting each other in the process. This in turn shaped the sort of leader I needed to be for that church.

It helps to know at least the basics of the story of which you are a part. To put it another way, the leader of a unique church needs to love his own church, warts and all, and stop imagining how much easier life would be if he led somebody else's church.

People's unique stories

The distinctive character of the local community and the church as a whole do not tell the whole story. Individuals have their own unique life-histories, and a unique church is built as a leader listens attentively to these stories. It is all too easy to see the church as an ecclesiastical sausage-machine. In practice, I have constantly been amazed by the variety of people who end up in particular churches, despite the label on the tin. People come to us with rich, diverse, confusing, awe-inspiring and messy stories. It is our privilege to listen to those stories and to God, to accompany individuals on the journey and help them discern the path ahead. Pat answers, simplistic solutions and rhetorical flourishes from the pulpit about complex personal and ethical issues simply won't do.

One of the intractable problems with a guardianship model of ministry is that it has a tendency to specify outcomes from the start, as well as to specify the path that must be taken to get there. A standardised vision for a church comes with an inbuilt risk that people's quirks, aberrations and uniqueness will be perceived as difficulties. To quote a line from a popular musical, 'How do you solve a problem like Maria?' In the musical, the answer to that question is that you don't force her into your own pet system or programme where she clearly does not fit. Instead, she needs to be liberated to be what God created her to be—and a key task of the church leader is to help her on a journey of discovery. Maybe the problem is not Maria but the way others try to pigeonhole her or co-opt her for their own big visions and systems. The era of the Spirit, said the prophet Joel, would be one in which ordinary people are empowered to dream dreams and see visions (Joel 2:28; Acts 2:17).

A big mistake of the 20th century was the systematic attempt to implement all-embracing systems and ideologies, such as Marxism and Fascism, into which people were expected to fit unquestioningly. The mute and compliant were hailed by the party faithful as heroes, and the creative thinkers and artists as enemies. All too often, religion worked on a similar model. As we have already noted, in many places it still does.

By contrast, a careful listening to people's individual stories is the pattern modelled by Jesus, as we see in the account of his conversations with the woman at the well (John 4:1–42) and the couple on the road to Emmaus (Luke 24:13–35). He gets alongside these people, listens for their agenda, affirms them, asks questions and tells stories, and gives space to respond in their own time.[9]

As we witness the death-throes of most of the '-isms' of the 20th century, the leader of the creative church needs to be not so much the importer of impressive systems and programmes, but a spiritual director.[10] In other words, she needs to listen to the real stories of real people, help them discern where God is in the fog, and help release their unique and God-given gifts.

Events

The British Prime Minister Harold Macmillan was once asked by a journalist what was most likely to blow a government off course. He memorably replied, 'Events, dear boy, events.' Many years later, all the parties in the 2010 British General Election had a manifesto of commitments they were hoping to implement if elected. As it turned out, no party gained an overall majority and the Conservatives and Liberal Democrats had to join forces in a coalition government. All the comprehensive plans and ideals that each party had worked so hard to agree had to be shelved, and a process of negotiating began. Events shaped outcomes.

Some things we simply cannot plan for, and an important test of leadership is our ability to respond quickly and appropriately to the unplanned and unpredictable. By definition, formulas, blueprints and programmes can never factor in these unforeseen events, but they are an essential part of Christian ministry in the real world. The question is whether we see them as a distraction from a predetermined plan or as the heart of our ministry—a problem or an opportunity.

In August 2004, a French student, Amélie Delagrange, was murdered on Twickenham Green, a few hundred metres from our front door. It was a deeply traumatic event for the local community, not least because there had been a string of other attacks locally, all on young women. Such moments can be a test of relevance and credibility for a local church. As quickly as we could, we arranged an open-air memorial service on the Green, to which local residents were invited. The service was not only a chance to pay a sad and shocked tribute to Amélie, but it constituted an expression of anger and a chance to reclaim the Green as a place of life and joy rather than death and fear. I visited the home where Amélie had been a lodger and I prayed with her landlady. We acknowledged the tragedy in our church services. I make no claim to have done these things particularly well, but at least we did something, and it gave our church a level of credibility in the area that a dozen programmes and courses could never have achieved.

The leader of the unique church needs the basic skills of the emergency services, a capacity to respond quickly and appropriately to the unforeseen. In other words, he needs to be flexible.

The biblical story

So is context everything? Are we to conclude that ministry in a unique and creative church is entirely responsive—to a local community and wider culture, the identity of the local church, people's unique stories, unforeseen events and the demands of the present moment? If so, the risk is that the context will set the agenda, and all elements of biblical faith that jar with the mood of the times are liable to be dropped as embarrassing and unpalatable.

The fact is that our local context is only part of the picture. The minister is also the one who is attentive to God's big story of human history, helps people find their own place in this wider narrative and allows scripture to ask challenging questions of our own culture. The Bible is not a collection of fragmentary pious meditations on people's spiritual lives. It is an inspired account of the meaning of history, from God's perspective, from beginning to end.[11] It identifies key themes and moments in history, which often turn out to bear little relation to the themes and moments identified in other accounts of history, such as the rise and fall of empires and the personal ambitions and rivalries of great men and women.

This is why the Christian faith must always subject other sources of guidance and authority to scripture. My own Anglican tradition has historically spoken of a three-legged stool of scripture, tradition and reason. Many leaders in the Anglican tradition today claim that all three carry equal weight, but this was never the intention of the formula, and cannot be right. If it is true that scripture offers, in any sense, a unique divine revelation of the shape of history and the purpose and crisis of human life, it must carry a different level of authority from tradition and reason. The latter are human activities, whose functions are in part to interpret and apply the priority of the Bible appropriately and intelligently. They clearly play a vital role but can never be considered as separate or rival sources of ultimate authority.[12] As Christians we take our lead from Jesus, who ascribed supreme authority to scripture.

When we speak of the authority of the Bible, we mean the authority of God, expressed through the Bible.[13] An essential role of the minister is to help people understand the story of their life in the light of God's bigger story. It is to help people make connections between their own lives on the one hand and the stories of the Bible and its resonant metaphors on the other—metaphors such as resurrection, exile, healing, desert, doubt, creation, homecoming and rescue.

The church leader is called to be a kind of structural engineer, building sound bridges between two worlds. In other words, she is a maker of connections.

Our historic roots

We must not only guard against a distortion of what the church believes, in the name of relevance. We must also guard against a distortion of what the church is called to be and do, in the name of pragmatism. A church that wants to connect in a culture of discontinuous change and numerical decline will be tempted to keep reinventing itself, to pursue an agenda of what works rather than what is true to its own roots and its own calling. If a particular style of service promotes a particular response or feeling in enough people, that fact alone can be seen as sufficient justification for its continuation.

But we belong to a church that has deep roots. There are core historic practices given or modelled by Jesus and the early church and honoured by two millennia of faithful practice. These include the two sacraments instituted by Jesus—baptism and Holy Communion—as well as corporate prayer, the laying on of hands, the public reading of scripture and the arts of spiritual direction and pastoral care. We are not only called to engage our culture in mission; we are also called to be stewards of the classic Christian tradition. We do not have to become a guardian of an inflexible model of ministry to recognise that the historic faith contains a number of core practices without which we lose our identity altogether.

One of the greatest gifts the church has to offer the world is a degree of irrelevance. It is the very oddness of a practice such as Holy Communion, its difference from everything else in our culture, that makes it strange and intriguing. If the church becomes as shallow, faddish and changeable as the culture, it no longer has anything distinctive to offer.

In AD327 the Emperor Constantine moved the capital of the Roman Empire from Rome to Constantinople (later Istanbul), with the explicit aim of founding a Christian city. For the first time, the Christian faith was moving from the margins to the centre. It was accorded social privileges instead of being persecuted, and Christianity became the official religion of the empire. Pagan temples were closed and churches built, church festivals were promoted, and being a Christian began to carry significant social prestige. The church started to become wealthy and clergy were exempted from paying taxes. It even reached the point where Constantine had to draw up legislation to stop rich men being ordained simply because they wanted to avoid paying taxes. In the fourth century, Christianity became entirely 'culturally relevant' to the society of its day. The tragedy was that this relevance came at great cost to the distinctiveness of the faith: Christianity and culture became so closely entwined that one was no longer separable from the other. The faith began to be compromised and diluted by the lure of success and power. The church jumped into bed with the culture and the era of Christendom had begun.[14]

Some believers, troubled by the compromises entailed in this newfound success and cultural relevance, headed off into the Egyptian desert to rediscover God by devoting themselves to prayer and solitude. The agenda of Anthony of Egypt and other hermits was one of devotion to God and a critical distance from culture. The chosen 'irrelevance' of these early Desert Fathers and Mothers (also including a formerly dissolute and promiscuous woman who became known as Mary of Egypt) meant that they found something distinctive to say to people from their culture. Large numbers of people flocked to them, out in the desert, to hear a word from God that was inaudible from within the culture.

Today, too, the church leader is called to safeguard a measure of healthy irrelevance to his surrounding culture. He is to be a keeper of the faith, a guardian of memories, a protector of life-giving roots.

An inherited tradition

We are not only custodians of the historic roots of the Christian faith. Each of us inherits a particular tradition, which generally carries a bundle of theological emphases, worship expectations and (for some of us) legal requirements set down in canon law. Few of us have the luxury of starting a congregation with a blank sheet of paper and the option of a wholesale reinvention of church in our own era. That may be the calling of a few pioneers, but it is not the weekly reality for most of us in leadership.

In practice, most of us will find ourselves pursuing uniqueness and creativity within the broad bounds of our own tradition. This itself, though, is an exciting and creative task: reimagining a tradition in changing times. Tradition is not the same as mindless traditionalism. As we have already noted, in a culture of superficiality and rapid change, a rediscovery of older, deeper roots will be one of our greatest assets in worship and mission. Witness the huge rise, in recent years, of people attending worship in the UK's cathedrals.

Some poets value the liberation of free verse, in which every new poem has a different shape. But historically, more poets have found liberation within the constraints of an existing form, such as the sonnet or haiku, and are energised by the prospect of creativity within clearly defined boundaries.

In 1960 the French writers Raymond Queneau and François le Lyonnais founded a group of writers called Oulipo. The distinctive of Oulipo is that all their works use what they called 'constrained writing' techniques. In other words, constraints are used as a means of sparking inspiration. These include traditional literary devices such as palindromes (where a word or phrase can be read in either direction, as in 'civic' or 'Was it a rat I saw?'), but the real creative workout in Oulipo lies in the invention of new constraints that spark new forms of creativity. George Perec's novel *La Disparition* is written entirely without the use of the letter 'e' (and its plot is a mystery that hangs around the disappearance of the letter 'e'); Queneau's *Exercises de Style* retells the same incident 99 times, but each account is different from the others in style.

Oulipo is simply an extreme example of what most writers know instinctively: limits are an aid to creativity rather than its enemy. Most authors choose to operate within a given genre (be it crime, romance, history, Bible study, farce, nature writing or any one of countless other styles), and they do so respecting the given conventions and expectations of that genre. Even authors who choose to subvert a genre do so in dialogue with its established rules. In literature, as in life, and as in worship, total freedom is rarely a condition of creativity.

To use a different sort of analogy, during the 1990s the Welsh screenwiter Russell T. Davies persuaded the BBC to allow him to revive the defunct family sci-fi series *Doctor Who*, whose decline had appeared terminal. When they agreed, Davies brilliantly plundered the earlier history of the series, keeping evil adversaries such as the Daleks and Cybermen, plus the Doctor's time machine, the Tardis, with its classic police box shape, and his sonic screwdriver. He even brought back actors from classic *Doctor Who* series, such as Elizabeth Sladen as Sarah Jane Smith.

Davies' genius was to reinvent a classic series for the 21st century in a way that was true to its historic roots but also felt fresh and exciting for a new generation. Davies has said that his biggest challenge was keeping the die-hard fans of *Doctor Who* on board with his reinvention of the Doctor. They were, after all, potentially his biggest allies and evangelists for the new series. Davies proved that it is possible both to satisfy the guardians of a tradition and to reach out and engage a completely new constituency with the same core tradition, creatively reinterpreted.

Russell T. Davies may well be the ideal role model for those of us who find ourselves called to minister in churches with a strong historic tradition and clearly defined expectations. Ours is a calling to exercise 'constrained ministry', but we can see this as a gift rather than a burden. We are being handed not the blank sheet of paper some of us might have dreamed of, but a Tardis, a sonic screwdriver and some Daleks, and we are invited to come up with a fresh, exciting new take on a classic theme.

In this lies profound hope for our historic denominations. My nine-year-old is a huge fan of *Doctor Who*, and his obsession with the current Doctor has led to his discovery of the earlier series on DVD, even the rather ropey 1980s incarnations (which have their own singular charm, not unlike much church culture, literature and song from the same era).

In this sense, many otherwise stimulating writers on creative ministry are surely wrong in one of their core assumptions. They assume that a vibrant, creative church can only emerge from the death of historic traditions. Allan Hirsch is the author of one of the most influential missional church books in recent years, *The Forgotten Ways*.[15] The book contains much that is insightful, but Hirsch idealises the new and unstructured and is consistently hostile to the institutional church and tradition, writing off the notion of time-honoured sacred space in historic buildings as 'spooky religious zones'. This is a particularly odd sideswipe, given the dramatic rise of interest in ancient patterns and places of spirituality, including practices drawn from the monastic movement, among a new generation.

Similarly, Erwin McManus of Mosaic in Los Angeles writes of the need for church leaders to be revolutionaries. According to McManus, we need to hold firm to the scriptures but loose to our traditions: 'Now we have to live with the reality that, all too many times, we kept our traditions and lost our children.'[16] As it stands, as a factual account of recent church history, this statement may well be true. Nevertheless, it fails to envisage another, more radical and creative option: that we may be able to keep both our traditions and our children. For this option to be a possibility, the church leader must have the confidence to be a reimaginer of tradition for a new generation.

Where the Spirit is at work

An eighth area to which the leader of the unique and creative church must be attentive is where the Spirit of God is already at work. A common assumption about evangelism is that we, the 'saved', have the gospel message, the presence of the Spirit and all the right answers—while they, the 'lost', have none of these. It is, then, our responsibility to take the gospel, the Spirit and the right answers into places where they are currently absent.

It would be more accurate to say that mission is about opening our eyes to where God's Spirit is already at work in our communities and trying to catch up with what God is already doing without us, often in the most unlikely places and people. 'The wind blows wherever it pleases,' said Jesus (playing on the fact that, in the Hebrew language, 'faith', 'wind', 'breath' and 'spirit' are all expressed by the same word, *ruach*). 'You hear its sound, but you cannot tell where it comes from or where it is going. So it is with everyone born of the Spirit' (John 3:8).

The idea that God goes ahead of us and is already at work in the hearts of all people, including the least likely, recurs as a biblical theme. All people are made in God's image and retain that image, even if it has been marred and neglected (Genesis 1:27). The Old Testament wisdom preacher says that God has 'set eternity' in the hearts of all people (Ecclesiastes 3:11). The inhabitants of the corrupt city of Nineveh turn out to be more ready to hear God's message than God's prophet, Jonah, is to tell them. Jesus says that nobody can come to him unless the Father draws them (John 6:44). Paul writes that all people retain a God-given conscience and an instinctive awareness of God, even if they choose to ignore them (Romans 1:20–21). At the heart of the gospel message is a clear understanding that God always takes the initiative: 'While we were still sinners, Christ died for us' (Romans 5:8); 'We love because he first loved us' (1 John 4:19).

Two related theological terms have been used to express some of these important biblical ideas. One is 'prevenient grace' (or simply 'prevenience'), which means the unexpected promptings of God in the lives of people who have no acknowledged faith. The other is 'common grace', the workings of God in the world and in the lives of all people, irrespective of their faith commitment. The term 'prevenient grace' has been particularly associated with the Methodist and Catholic traditions, and 'common grace' with the Reformed tradition. Both are surely true.

Whichever part of the church we belong to, it can only energise and enrich our outreach if we realise that God is already out there, getting on with the job. Every encounter, every conversation we have with the people on our doorstep, is an opportunity to discover what the Spirit is already stirring up in their lives. Most people will be unable to articulate it in those terms, yet most will be able to identify feelings such as a restlessness with their life, a sense that there must be 'something more', a desire for community and belonging, a sense that they want a solid framework of values to hand on to their children, a strange feeling that they are being drawn to a God they don't believe in or a church they profess to despise, big questions about meaning and purpose, or an unexpected sense of the spiritual or mysterious.

The task of the minister is to be a patient birdwatcher, binoculars at the ready, looking out for the telltale signs of the presence of a dove (Matthew 3:16) and the arrival of a wild goose (said to have been the symbol of the Spirit in the Celtic church). In other words, she has to keep her eyes open to what is already happening all around her. To return to the image with which we began this section on eight-way attentiveness, there are already leopards hiding in the suburbs. Most of us just haven't seen them yet, because we haven't been looking for them.

Unique combination

These, I am convinced, are eight key areas to which any church leader needs to be attentive, not just those considering a church plant or setting up a fresh expression. But if all church leaders pay attention to the same criteria, will we not all come up with similar solutions? Quite the opposite. The whole point of this model is that it leads to unique and creative outcomes. Guardianship models of church tend to specify blueprints to which any church should conform, whatever and wherever that church is. The destination is known in advance, the route clear and well-mapped.

The model of attentiveness to a local context is precisely about throwing away other people's success stories and formulas. It is about learning what sort of questions to ask in my own unique setting, with these unique people, at this unique moment in time. The questions each leader asks may be the same sort of questions, but we each ask them to different people and places. I might ask a roomful of 30 people to tell me their names, and I will get 30 different answers. A detective might follow an identical procedure for taking the fingerprints of those same 30 people, and every fingerprint will be different from all the others. We ask identical questions and apply identical tests in different settings precisely to discover that which is unique.

No other church leader can engage the particular combination of place and people that I do at this moment in the earth's history. I have a unique calling and unique opportunities. So what do I, as a leader, do with this information? Is this attentiveness something that I do alone, with an inner group, or as a whole church? How might it affect what we actually do on Sundays, or during the week? We shall explore these questions in due course, but first we need to take a look at another of the variables, a ninth form of attentiveness. Not only are the church and local setting unique at a unique moment in time. So is the leader.

──────────────── ✳ ────────────────

Snapshot: Cake on a Wednesday

When the Revd Andrew Jones* became vicar of Llanbedrog, a seaside village near Pwllheli in north Wales, the post had been vacant for three years. The congregation was in steep decline and there were no parish activities other than a Sunday morning service, after which most people would promptly head off home.

Andrew wondered if a short weekday service might provide an alternative focus for worship and fellowship among the largely retired local population. During his first Lent in the parish, he tried out a simple 30-minute service, without hymns, sermon or offering. The service drew a small but committed core membership who decided to continue meeting after Easter, with the addition of coffee after the service.

A second Lent arrived and Andrew suggested that the group might begin to study the Bible together. They initially tried holding this study on a Tuesday evening, but it was a dismal failure as nobody wanted to come out in the evening: people preferred daytime activities. Somebody suggested moving the Bible study to a Wednesday afternoon, the same day as the weekday service. The cynic in Andrew wondered whether this was so that the congregation could 'get it all over in a day', but it turned out to be an inspired decision.

The group started with John's Gospel, which they all found fascinating. This was a new experience to everybody who came, and their enthusiasm inspired Andrew to continue the experiment. As Andrew's second Christmas came round, a member of the group suggested they all have lunch together in the art gallery restaurant near the church. The group took a Christmas

* *A different Andrew Jones from the one at Grace Church Hackney!*

break, but when they came back in the new year they continued to have lunch together, sometimes in the art gallery restaurant, sometimes in the pub or garden centre, sometimes in the church itself.

After two years, Wednesday had become the highlight of local parish life, involving a service, a good lunch out and a stimulating Bible study, along with the chance to get to know one's neighbours better. Fifteen years on, this pattern still continues. The pattern for a typical Wednesday is that at 9.30am a CD of contemplative music is played in church, and many parishioners come for a time of quiet reflection. At 10am there is a Communion service in church, now with an unaccompanied hymn. After this comes coffee, and most of those attending head off together for lunch. The group reassembles at 1pm for tea and home-made cake (but never, stresses Andrew, merely a packet of biscuits), and a time for chat. At 2pm they begin their Bible study together, and it all ends by 3.30pm. Approximately 40 attend in the morning, of whom 30 return for the afternoon session. They have completed studies of all the books of the New Testament and ten from the Old Testament, and particular favourites have been the Gospel of John and the book of Exodus.

Wednesday has become Andrew's favourite day of the week, and he says he has learned so much about the Bible, himself, group dynamics, people and—ultimately—the grace of God.

5

Unique leader

Goths in Australia

One day I was chatting to a group of parents at our link primary school in Strawberry Hill about the fashions and styles we adopted in our younger days. One mum confided that in her teenage years she used to be a Goth. She had dyed black hair and wore a huge black overcoat and heavy make-up. The problem was that she grew up in Australia, where the sunny climate was less than conducive to the gloomy pallor of Goth culture. The whole of her teenage years were spent feeling swelteringly hot, draped in layers of black clothing, under the fierce Australian sun. That is the reason, she added, why antipodean Goths always look red-faced.

There is something endearing about teenagers wanting to find their 'true' identity and trying out the persona of somebody they admire. They want to dress like that character and adopt their ways of talking and attitudes, be they a musician, film star or sports personality, even if the image is clearly ill-fitting for the young person in question. But it is not just impressionable teenagers who love to emulate those they admire. I remember one old Methodist minister who grew his hair so that he would look like his hero John Wesley. Back in the 1980s I watched several young leaders in independent charismatic churches develop the mannerisms and preaching style of a prominent New Church leader. In London church circles it is possible to recognise a St Helen's Bishopsgate or Holy Trinity Brompton look and style of preaching. Leaders model themselves, consciously or unconsciously, on role models within their own tradition. If mischievous aliens were simultaneously to abduct ministers from the Pentecostal Kensington Temple, the Anglo-Catholic All Saints Margaret Street and the liberal, socially active St James Piccadilly, and drop them back in a Sunday morning service in each other's churches, the results would be as unsettling as abducting zoo animals and dropping them back in the wrong cages.

It is easy to smile at ministerial and priestly stereotypes, but the desire to emulate an admired mentor has strong biblical precedent. In ancient Israel, the way students would learn was literally to follow their teacher (rabbi) around, do what he did, look the way he looked and imitate him in everything. The students would one day become rabbis themselves, so they received a comprehensive on-the-job training based on close emulation. One day, in turn, they would have their own crowd of students following them. The word for these students, who followed their teacher round, was 'disciples'.

For such a time as this

The biblical experience of discipling leaders into an established tradition is balanced by another vital emphasis—that God calls unique leaders with unique skills for unique times. Esther stepped forward to help avert the genocide of her people; Moses led his people from slavery in Egypt; Nehemiah led the rebuilding of the walls of Jerusalem; Paul pioneered mission to the Gentiles.

In the book of Esther, Mordecai recognises the strategic nature of Esther's position in the royal court, asking her, 'Who knows but that you have come to royal position for such a time as this?' (Esther 4:14). This has become something of a cliché in revivalist circles in recent years, but it remains a good verse to help church leaders remember the distinctives of their calling. We too are in the place where we are 'for such a time' as our own day, and we bring a unique mix of gifts, aptitudes and foibles to the tasks we face. Not only is my church and context unique: I am unique, too. This uniqueness is a combination of a number of 'givens' about myself, as well as aspects of my life that are beyond my control and choices I have made down the years.

Below are some of the variables that make me who I am and make my ministry unique. Inevitably, there may be some degree of overlap between sections.

Gender, ethnicity and age

At the most basic level, I have a gender and ethnicity and I am a particular age. My maleness or femaleness, my appearance and skin colour, the cultures that have shaped me, and how old I am, will have a profound impact on the sort of ministry I exercise. These variables may also determine, in subtle ways, others' responses to my ministry, where I choose to exercise that ministry and whether certain doors are opened or closed to me.

Upbringing and life experience

I grew up in a particular place, or number of places, surrounded by particular groups of people who held certain attitudes and assumptions about the world. I may have subsequently left those people, places and attitudes behind or I may have continued to embrace all of them. Either way, for better or worse, they will have left their mark on me, as will the experiences I have had through my adult life to date—achievements and setbacks alike. Some moments and experiences will stand out to me as achievements that brought particular satisfaction, even if they may not seem significant to other people. It is worth taking time to reflect on these experiences and discern what it was that made them particularly satisfying. Similarly, there will have been moments of acute pain caused by events, my own failings or wounds inflicted by others. It may well be that we can be most helpful to others in areas where we have struggled ourselves.

Similarly, all of us grew up with some sort of attitude towards faith, even if it was an attitude of indifference or hostility. I may have grown up in a church tradition that I now view from a critical distance, or affirm wholeheartedly, or remember with a shudder. I will probably have seen a particular type of church leadership modelled, along with a particular way to lead services, preach and relate to church members. My faith background will inevitably have influenced the person I am today. It is likely to influence the sort of church where I feel at home and the expectations I have of the church where I minister. Somehow I found my way to the particular church tradition and denomination with which I identify, and that itself will set certain assumptions and expectations about the shape of my ministry.

Temperament and team role

In psychology, temperament denotes those aspects of our personality that are generally accepted to be innate rather than learned or chosen. They include introversion and extraversion—in other words, whether a person is energised primarily by reflection and time away from other people or by action and interaction with others. Such a distinction is likely to influence significantly the sort of ministry in which we will thrive or struggle. The distinction between introvert and extravert is central to the influential Myers-Briggs Type Indicator (MBTI™) for analysing personality. Its other categories are to do with whether we tend to gather information in practical or intuitive ways; whether we make decisions more on the basis of rational thought or empathy with people; and whether we prefer to live in a structured or spontaneous way. Personality inventories such as MBTI™ can be a useful tool to help us understand ourselves and the way we relate to the outside world.

Other psychological tests focus more on characteristics such as whether I am a naturally cooperative or competitive person, whether I prefer high-risk or low-risk situations, whether I like change or resist it, whether I prefer to work alone or in a team, and whether I like a steady routine or variety.[1] If we go with the grain of our God-given personality, we are more likely to find fulfilment in our work. A leader who is a perfectionist may find it frustrating to work in a setting where most people lead disorganised and chaotic lives, or, equally, she may find this an ideal outlet for her desire to bring order. Self-awareness and honesty with ourselves and others is key.

Similarly, the Belbin Team Role Inventory analyses the different sorts of roles people play in the context of a team. For those of us who work in teams, this provides the context for the exercise of our individual skills and interests, and it is unrealistic to consider individual abilities in isolation from the setting in which they will be put to use. Belbin's categories include the Plant, the 'absent-minded professor' type, who is good at generating creative and unorthodox ideas; the Completer-Finisher, the perfectionist who sees a job through to the end in every detail; and the Coordinator, the confident chairperson. Again, it can be helpful for the leader with a team of staff or volunteers to give some thought to the dynamics of that team, and where he personally fits most comfortably. A little reflection and discussion in this area can help prevent misunderstandings and conflict later.

Skills and gifts

I have particular talents and abilities—some that come naturally to me, and others that I have worked at. In some areas I will have received specialist training. I will have my own distinctive 'voice' for preaching, which may be quite different from that of other preachers of my own tradition or other traditions. Generally speaking, I will be most effective if I work in my areas of natural and acquired strength, and those areas where I am most skilled give a good indication of where I will find most satisfaction in ministry. It may well be that others can advise on where they think I am most gifted: we are not always the best judge of our own skills.

Desires and ambitions

Nobody else has the same mix of desires and ambitions that I have. What is it that excites me and makes me want to get up in the morning? What is the cause for which I am happy to work tirelessly? What is my dream? These are positive motivators which should influence how and where we minister. But it is also as well to be honest about any hidden motives for my ambitions, the less than noble factors that may be driving me. Might there be an element of wanting to be seen to be successful, wanting to be needed, wanting power over others, or wanting to minister with particular people or in a particular place because it will reflect well on myself? We may never fully unravel our mixture of motives, but it is worth asking ourselves some hard questions before our dubious drivers cause harm to ourselves and others.

Many actors, musicians and models choose a 'stage' name that communicates a particular identity to the general public. Similarly, since the sixth century, most Popes have chosen a 'regnal' name in honour of a predecessor or saint whom they hold in high esteem. If you were asked to choose a ministry name for yourself, what would it be, and what would your chosen name say about your passions and priorities in ministry?

The settings that fascinate and infuriate me

Each of us has settings that we find fascinating or offputting. Some love the buzz of the big city, some the intimacy of a small rural community, while others feel at home in the suburbs. This in turn is linked to whether I am more attracted by a specialist or a generalist type of ministry. Urban ministers are more likely to be leading a single church of a particular churchmanship, to which people are happy to travel for the particular 'brand' on offer. In rural areas, by contrast, clergy are more likely to lead a number of churches, which may be of varying shades of tradition, and local people are more likely to worship at their local church, which means that rural churches tend to be less extreme in their worship traditions. Similarly, rural ministers generally need to be broader and more accommodating of the *status quo*, and more cautious about sudden and dramatic change.

During our time in Twickenham, my most controversial decision was to disband the old choir and eventually facilitate the development of a larger, more occasional group of singers. It had become clear to me and other people over a period of time that the dominance of services by the choir was a major hindrance to new people attending. This proved to be an explosive step (I referred to it afterwards as 'pressing the nuclear button'), and some people left in anger. But I took the decision, confident that in the west London suburbs many more people would prefer the new style of service and start attending—which they did. Had I pressed the same 'nuclear button' in a rural area, the chances are that I would have alienated not only the choir but also their friends in the congregation, and the rest of the village would have stayed away in protest, so I would have ended up with an empty church. A different approach would have been needed in a different setting.

We are most likely to find fulfilment in our work if we can draw on our natural preferences. We must, of course, be open to the challenge to go beyond our comfort zones, to hear the sort of call that comes to a Jonah, a Daniel or a St Patrick. There are occasions when church leaders are called to minister in exile, to 'sing the songs of the Lord while in a foreign land' (Psalm 137:4). This may mean that they find themselves some distance from home, or they may be very close to home geographically but worlds away from home in terms of culture and demographics. In the absence of clear and specific guidance to minister in a situation of exile, however, it is likely that God will go with the grain of what fascinates and excites us. We are more likely to minster effectively in a setting that energises us.

At the same time, even those settings and situations that infuriate us might also be a pointer to where we can minister most effectively. Bill Hybels writes helpfully of a 'holy discontent' that motivates a leader to get things done, an anger or frustration that refuses to allow a given situation to continue unchallenged. This holy discontent, says Hybels, may well be part of our calling from God.[2]

The people who fascinate and infuriate me

Are there particular groups of people I feel drawn towards and others I find more challenging? Are there people of a particular age whom I love to be around or struggle to connect with? Some will be aware of a concern to help ex-offenders, students, those who are ill, older people, artists or sports people. These natural preferences are likely to give a good indication of where I will minister most effectively.

My APEPT ministry

Ephesians 4:11 outlines the core ministries that are foundational for any church. There are five key roles that any church needs, and God calls and equips members of the church to fulfil these roles. The letter to the Ephesians does not limit these ministries to clergy and other church leaders, and does not say that these are the five roles that should be exercised by all church leaders. Quite the opposite. The context comes in 4:7: 'To each one of us grace [or 'a special gift'] has been given as Christ apportioned it.' The letter says that each member has received a portion of grace in one of five different roles, that there are five basic types of people in the church and that each type contributes something to its life and work. Although these ministry types are not limited to those of us in church leadership, leaders are certainly included in 'each one of us'.

Together, the five ministries are sometimes known by the acronym formed by their initial letters, APEPT:

- **A**postle: A pioneer or innovator with fresh ideas and an ability to start up new ministries.
- **P**rophet: A person who listens to God, discerns situations with wisdom and speaks out when needed.
- **E**vangelist: A person concerned to connect with people outside the faith. This person may have natural gifts for befriending others and explaining the faith.
- **P**astor: One who draws alongside people to nurture and care for them. The pastor may well have a gift of hospitality and a good listening ear.
- **T**eacher: Somebody who is passionate about explaining the faith and expounding the scriptures.

It may be that we have strengths in more than one of these areas, but Ephesians indicates that one will resonate in a special way for each of us. How do I discern which of these roles should characterise my ministry? Useful questions to ask might include: Which of these areas excites and energises me? In which of these ministries have I already been effective? Which of the five would the people I know and trust most identify with me? An awareness of which of these roles I am particularly equipped to fulfil will not only help me play to my strengths in ministry, it will also help me value and draw on the gifts of others with different strengths in leadership positions.

My spiritual pathway

For any church leader, an obvious priority is to safeguard our intimacy with God. That said, it is important to realise that there is no one-size-fits-all model when it comes to personal spirituality. We can each feel free to encounter God in one or more of a range of ways, without trying to follow somebody else's path. Some of us are drawn closer to God in silence, others in activity; some indoors, others in the natural world; some by study, others by exuberant praise; some through pattern and ritual, others through spontaneity; some through simplicity and withdrawal, others by engaging with contemporary culture. We should never covet the spiritual walk of the next person. We each need to love God as we can, not as we can't.

Even our patterns of sin and shortcomings can be distinctive to us. Our unique temperament, culture, family background and gender are likely to predispose each of us to what Michael Mangis, Professor of Psychology at Wheaton College, Illinois, describes as our 'signature sin'.[3] Our sins are not random: they are distinctive to each of us and grow out of unchosen aspects of who we are, plus choices we have made in the past. There is much to be gained from identifying and naming our signature sins, probably with the help of a friend, mentor or spiritual director, and from identifying resources that will help us. These might include spiritual practices and disciplines, communities, and rhythms of life. The dangers for church leaders who fail to name their signature sin and find help and support in dealing with it are all too evident.

What recharges my batteries

There are two main models for recharging batteries. The small batteries used in radios, clocks and toy cars need to be taken out of their appliances from time to time and recharged in a battery charger plugged into the mains electricity. In a car, however, the battery is charged by the alternator while the engine is running. Both types of recharging have direct application to Christian ministry.

There are times when we need to withdraw from active service for holidays. We need to guard regular time off, on a sabbath-rest principle, and build in time for exercise and simply having fun, which can easily be squeezed out by the demands of ministry. We also need to be intentional about booking time away from the church—such as retreats, conferences, cell groups of colleagues, and study time that recharges our batteries.

Recharging can also involve time away from the nine-to-five, spent with others who have a similar perspective on ministry. This, incidentally, is the real value of networks of like-minded leaders and events such as New Wine, Fulcrum, Affirming Catholicism or the Willow Creek Association. As we have explored, we should not look to these groups for ready-made solutions to specific local questions. Ministry should be about looking for unique and creative solutions in our own context, which may be quite different from those required elsewhere. The real value of such networks is the fellowship and support they provide from people with a broadly similar outlook. They should be a support for our own creativity rather than a refuge from it. Only you will know what pattern of 'removal from the appliance' recharging will best top up your depleted energies.

At the same time, the alternator model of recharging also applies to church leaders: our battery can be recharged as we drive. It is important that our working week contains at least some activities that excite and energise us, otherwise we can find ourselves reduced to responding to other people's agendas and being ground down by the tyranny of the urgent. After a while, the joy and creativity of ministry can ebb away entirely. If this is a risk, as it is for most of us, it is important to block out in our diary at least some time each week to do those activities that give us life and energy rather than exhaust and demoralise us.

Admitting who I am

A few years back, I attended a seminar for church leaders on church growth. During the coffee break I got chatting to another of the clergy attending, a young man from the Anglo-Catholic tradition. He was silent and thoughtful after the session, and eventually confided that he found it all profoundly depressing. He could not relate to any of the evangelistic strategies being outlined by the speaker. I asked what he did feel able to do in his parish. His response was gloomy and downhearted: 'Just the obvious stuff that all vicars do.' When I asked what he meant by that, he replied, 'Oh, pastoral care, home visits, visits to hospitals and hospices, praying with older people.'

As it happened, he enjoyed these pastoral roles and found them energising, but the effect of the seminar was to make him feel that these 'mundane' aspects of ministry were second-rate or old-hat. It had not occurred to him that these roles might be part of his distinctive personal make-up, that many other church leaders might not feel any great call to the pastoral ministry and that, in New Testament terms, 'pastor' is only one of five roles identified as vital to church growth and health. He was genuinely astonished when I confided that my own role involved few pastoral encounters and that (at the time) I felt little by way of calling or desire to be a pastor. It had been no significant part of my own call to ordained ministry, which had been more to do with communication. I added that it was likely that his own method of church growth would be to provide a warm, caring environment in which local people felt loved and nurtured. In the anonymous London suburb where he ministered, that was an extraordinary gift. His calling might not be to pioneer evangelism courses or organise large outreach events, but simply to love people.

A penny seemed to drop for him that day. It was nothing to do with the presentation on the latest techniques for evangelism. It happened in an accidental conversation over coffee, with the realisation that God wanted him not to be somebody else but to be himself, to follow his own calling and not the next person's. Ministry is the coming together of a unique church in a unique neighbourhood at a unique moment in time, led by a unique minister. We should never wish away that uniqueness or feel inadequate as we compare ourselves to another leader.

Honesty on the journey

Finally, it is worth remembering that people, even church leaders, change over the years. I am not the same person that I was as a teenager or when I first entered ministry. A lot of water has passed under the bridge and, as the Greek philosopher Heraclitus pointed out, you cannot step twice into the same river.

It is all too easy to carry through life an image of ourselves that was formed when we were young adults, desperate to bolster our insecure identity—an image that may have owed a great deal to our upbringing and to our friends and church from that time. We will be of most help as leaders if we can be honest with ourselves and others about who we are and who we are becoming. In some cases, this might involve the honesty to leave behind a self-image, attitudes, priorities and a spiritual path which are now as ill-fitting and anachronistic as a set of clothes I wore in my youth. In other cases, it will involve the honesty to admit that we should leave a current post, which might once have seemed right. I can think of at least three situations I have known where a church leader should clearly have left much sooner. In each case, they ended up staying for between ten and 20 years. The result was misery for the clergy in question and an unedifying combination of stagnation and decline for their churches.

This kind of brutal honesty about ourselves and our ministries might feel unsettling and risky, but self-awareness is crucial if we are to practise the ninth attentiveness: to myself as a unique leader.

Snapshot: The Guitar Club

In 2008, three inner-city Church of England churches in the Aston area of Birmingham were joined together as the parish of Aston and Nechells. The vicar of Aston Parish Church, Andy Jolley, became vicar of the new combined parish, which is in an Urban Priority Area, multicultural and predominantly poor. At the end of that same year, a new curate, Beverley Watson, joined the team.

Beverley's previous work experience had included many years teaching music, particularly piano and French horn. She found that as she was getting to know members of the three congregations, no less than five people happened to mention that they would love to learn to play the guitar. Even though the guitar was not Beverley's main instrument, she was a competent guitarist and decided to set up a Guitar Club. She recruited another guitarist from one of the churches to help her, along with the husband of the Deanery Missioner, who also played. The first Guitar Club opened its doors in September 2010, with twelve members from an astonishing diversity of backgrounds, including Caribbean, Nigerian, Lithuanian, Georgian and Polish, with ages ranging from 10 to 70. Several were asylum seekers who had only just been granted UK residence, and a couple of people brought friends who had no church connections.

Beverley aimed to teach the group six chords and six songs in six weeks, which was the tagline for her advance publicity. After ten weeks, club members had learnt four chords and four songs. But Beverley reflected that as most had never held an instrument before, and English was a second language for many, this was good progress. On Advent Sunday 2010, eight members of the group joined the band at Aston Parish Church for a great celebration service. Immediately afterwards they dedicated themselves to learning a further two chords and three more songs in time for the Contemporary Christmas Carol Service.

The Guitar Club has been a good learning experience for Beverley. She says it has helped her realise the vital importance of listening to what people are saying, and responding to their requests. The club has been a great way to build community among a disparate group of people with few relationships or footholds in the UK. It has drawn in people who would otherwise have had no connection with a local church. It is starting to give people skills for which they are grateful, and it is also strengthening the musical capacity of churches in the team.

Other local churches soon began to ask if they could come on board and bring some of their people, and other members of the parish started asking if the course could be run again. At the time of writing, Beverley continues to nurture and teach the members of the first Guitar Club.

6

Rethinking vision

Vision and goals

Can we ever know the destination before we have begun the journey? Much management theory would say that this is not only possible, it is imperative. The logic seems clear and compelling: we need to have a clear sense of where we are going to end up, otherwise how will we know if we are heading in the right direction? We need to have a clear vision of our destination and set clear goals in order to reach it.

The model of vision that has predominated in business and some church circles in the late 20th and early 21st centuries has been essentially a top-down model. The Chief Executive Officer (CEO) of a company, or senior pastor of a church, has the key visionary role. He is the one with the skills and imagination to see a better future for the corporation or church, and the whole company is then shaped around that vision. On this model of leadership, the leader is essentially the initiator and keeper of a big vision, which cascades down through the rest of the organisation. This big vision will involve a compelling picture of the organisation as it could be in, say, five, ten or 30 years' time, and ambitious goals are set in order to progress towards this destination, goals that are usually required to be SMART—Specific, Measurable, Attainable, Realistic and Time-Bound.

This business model has been widely adopted in the church. One enthusiast is Bill Hybels of Willow Creek, near Chicago. The most systematic and autobiographical account of his leadership approach can be found in his book *Courageous Leadership*. Hybels underlines the importance of clear vision, which he describes as a 'compelling picture of the future that enables us to say, "We know our destination. Nothing will lure us off the path from here to there. We will not be distracted."'[1]

The structure of the book underlines the importance of visionary leadership. After an introduction, Hybels' first substantive chapter is on vision, 'the leader's most potent weapon', followed by a chapter on goal setting and strategic planning. He describes the process of setting a vision for Willow Creek and then setting specific goals to help the church achieve that vision. In the first instance, goals included increasing attendance at their weekend services from 15,000 people to 20,000, and the number of churches around the world linked to their Willow Creek Association network from 1400 to 6000.

Popular leadership guru (and ordained Methodist minister) John Maxwell is likewise convinced that a business model of vision carries over well into church leadership, and similarly assumes that the main visionary is the minister as CEO:

Vision is everything for a leader. It is utterly indispensable. Why? Because vision leads the leader. It paints the target. It sparks and fuels the fire within, and draws him forward. It is also the fire lighter for those who follow that leader. Show me a leader without vision, and I'll show you someone who isn't going anywhere. At best, he is traveling in circles.[2]

I look back over notes from church leaders' events I attended throughout the 2000s, including Willow Creek Global Leadership summits and Vineyard conferences, and am reminded of the extent to which vision became a dominant theme throughout this period. The unspoken assumption was that visionary leadership for the church ought to be fundamentally the same kind of top-down vision modelled by the most dynamic businesses of the day. Emphases at these conferences included the importance of the leader's discerning a big vision, keeping the vision clear and focused, stopping vision from 'leaking', and communicating vision regularly to staff, and the urgency of reinforcing the big vision through all ministries in our churches.

This influx of management terminology into the church has polarised church leaders. Some have welcomed the shift with enthusiasm, particularly those who have long reacted against the traditional stereotype of clergy as caring but ultimately rather aimless pastors, 'at best travelling in circles'. They are more than happy to replace the image of the old-fashioned, bumbling vicar with the heroic and visionary leader celebrated in the business world, management textbooks and inspirational autobiographies. Father Ted and Reverend Timms (of 'Postman Pat' fame) are no match for the thrusting entrepreneurs of TV series such as 'Dragon's Den' and 'The Apprentice'.

Others, however, have resented all intrusion of business models into church leadership and, in particular, question the model of pastor as a visionary CEO. Let's be honest: in some cases this resentment may well stem from an instinctive cultural conservatism and a sentimental attachment to inherited models of ministry in which an earlier generation of ministers were trained. This kind of knee-jerk resistance to change by traditionalists does not help to progress the important debate about the role of today's clergy. The fact remains that any organisation which has lost 'market share' in the spectacular manner of the churches in the UK and Europe in recent decades would be foolish in the extreme not to take a fresh look at the leadership style that has presided over the decline. Studies in leadership theory and skills have been a welcome addition to the curricula of many theological colleges and a required part of on-the-job clergy training in some dioceses and church networks, and the new focus on mission action planning in parishes can only be a good thing.

Deeper questions remain, though, about whether business models should be imported wholesale into the church. Now that top-down models of visionary leadership are increasingly being questioned in the business world, it is timely to reassess both their effectiveness and their appropriateness in the church, and that is the aim of this chapter. To underline: we are not questioning the value of purpose, focus, strategy, intentionality, clear communication and so on in church leadership. These are all desirable. We are questioning the effectiveness and appropriateness of the CEO model of vision that has been adopted in so many sectors of today's church.

Visions and blueprints

One characteristic of a classic CEO model of vision is that the vision for the organisation becomes predetermined, at least for a few years. In the words of Bill Hybels, the destination is fixed. A blueprint of a better future is glimpsed by a visionary leader, who then communicates it to others and takes them with him on the journey to the fixed destination. Leaders well-versed in management theory will paint a clear picture of where their particular church could be in a few years' time, and will work with other leaders to break this picture down into specific goals to enable the church to realise the vision.

Other leaders might not use the language of vision but will have a blueprint of the ultimate destination in mind which is every bit as specific as a classic CEO, top-down vision. Their own blueprint of the future may be shaped by their church tradition, the college or church in which they were trained, their own temperament and where they personally find spiritual sustenance and renewal. This blueprint in the mind of the leader—overt or implicit—in turn shapes the core assumptions and expectations of her church.

With apologies to Rick Warren's *Purpose-Driven Church*, here are a few church blueprints I have known down the years and still encounter regularly. As well as indicating the blueprint that motivates them, I add a few question marks of my own about each model.

The Surplice-Driven Church

This is the church or cathedral whose blueprint is a particular model of perfection in vestments, liturgy, choreography and choral music. It is a church that sees itself as a centre of aesthetic excellence and has clear benchmarks from within its tradition to identify when this excellence is achieved. It is likely to employ lay staff with a strong track record of professionalism in their field rather than clear evidence of Christian devotion. Paid members of the choir will invariably be superb singers but may well have little interest in questions of faith. Ordained leaders may be selected, in large part, for their ability to orchestrate the aesthetics of the occasion.

Excellent liturgy and ceremonial can facilitate a powerful entering into the drama of the gospel, and such services can act as a window into the awesomeness of God for many people. However, ritual alone can never be an ultimate destination for a church. To have integrity, any fine music and ritual that people encounter in our churches must be an authentic expression of faith, discipleship and mission. Without these, worship becomes just another concert, and the church just another highbrow arts venue. The same principle can apply every bit as much at the cutting edge of charismatic church worship as in traditional styles: professionalism can become an end in itself; a flawless professionalism takes over.

In our generation, the decline of traditional cookery skills has coincided with a dramatic rise in celebrity chefs with TV series and lavishly illustrated books. The contribution of celebrity chefs ought to be to inspire the rest of us to make something creative and delicious ourselves. All too often, though, watching becomes a substitute for doing. Cookery was never intended to be a spectator sport in which the de-skilled sit back and admire the virtuosity of the professional. Nor was worship.

The Papoose-Driven Church

This is the church whose aim is giving birth to new Christians. Its overriding aim is conversion, and, as soon as new members are converted, it is made clear that their aim in turn is to convert others. The passion of such churches for mission is commendable, but, as an ultimate purpose for a church, conversion alone is as bizarre as saying that the only purpose of being alive is to produce more new lives. That begs obvious questions such as 'Yes, but what is life actually *for*?' and 'What do I *do* now I'm alive?' In Christian terms, those questions are 'What am I being saved *for*?' and 'What do I *do* now I'm a believer?'

The message heard by converts in such churches is often that this life—the earth, culture, science, the arts, spiritual practices and our human relationships—is unimportant in itself, that life is no more than a waiting room for heaven and our only calling is to pull more people into the waiting room. This is a strange distortion of the biblical vision, which is cosmic and purposeful in scope and has to do with the healing of the world—the reconciliation of our present alienation from God, each other and the planet. It is, in the words of Jesus, about living life to the full (John 10:10).

In fact, the Papoose-Driven Church sometimes even manages to misunderstand the one biblical theme it claims to value. Its members often speak of salvation as the rescue of individual souls out of the world. Biblical images of salvation, however, focus much more on the restoration of relationships, leading to an ultimate healing of the nations and the cosmos. If I personally am healed, it is so that I am better able to take part in the healing of creation. Salvation does not begin or end with individuals. It is about wholeness and community, not solitary escape. A big, holistic understanding of salvation answers those crucial questions about what life is ultimately for.

The Soundness-Driven Church

The Soundness-Driven Church's blueprint is purity of doctrine and teaching within a particular tradition of Bible exposition. The focus of worship is on the all-important sermon, and small groups major on Bible study with a view to helping members attain soundness of belief. All credit to them. In the New Testament Paul alerts his young colleague Timothy to the importance of holding to the truth and warns of a day coming when people will follow their own whims and preferences rather than sound doctrine (2 Timothy 4:2–4).

But soundness alone can never provide a blueprint for a church. While it provides important parameters for belief, soundness of doctrine alone does not guarantee spiritual passion or discipleship. Jesus' own summary of what matters most in life centres on loving God and loving people (Matthew 22:34–40), and is echoed in Paul's list of the fruit of the Spirit (Galatians 5:22–23). This is a picture of a worthwhile destination. Sound doctrine offers, at best, a signpost that points in the right direction. When sound doctrine becomes a goal in itself, those who obsess about finer points of doctrine can develop a tendency towards judgmentalism and humourlessness.

Some years back, my wife and I visited a central London church with a formidable reputation for solid biblical preaching. Sure enough, the sermon dominated the proceedings. The preacher that evening used the letters of the word ISRAEL as an acronym to give us a range of angles on how sinful we are in the eyes of God. Letter by letter, he expounded biblical themes of sin with grim thoroughness. We were convinced that, by the letter L, he might lighten up and end with Love—without which, says Paul, our faith is a waste of time (1 Corinthians 13). Unfortunately not. L turned out to stand for 'Less Excuse'. We Christians had 'less excuse' than everybody else for our sinfulness. And that was it: sound as a pound, but miserable as sin. Nobody cracked a smile the whole time; nobody welcomed or spoke to us. We went home wondering precisely how such a gospel was supposed to be 'good news' to anybody.

There is a further difficulty for the church that views soundness of doctrine as its sole aim: it is unlikely to communicate effectively in today's climate. Nobody is interested in disembodied doctrines. What people are looking for is a better way to live, something earthed and practical. Christianity is far more than dogma, but you would not know it from sitting in a Soundness-Driven Church. Sound doctrine is good, but those who pursue it most doggedly seem vulnerable to ignoring key emphases in the very Bible they purport to defend, and their obsession with minutiae of biblical exegesis can hinder the biblical call to mission that they purport to follow.

The Furnace-Driven Church

This is the church whose blueprint is revival, an overwhelming sense of the presence of God over a concentrated period of time, in which people experience extraordinary phenomena and huge numbers are converted. The leaders and members of such churches are driven by memories of earlier eras of revival, such as the Welsh revival of 1904–05, the Azusa Street revival of Los Angeles in 1906 (which gave rise to today's global Pentecostalism), the Hebridean revival of the mid-20th century and the East African revival of the 1930s. The leader of the Furnace-Driven Church may well be a self-professed 'storm chaser' who flies around the world to experience current revivals first-hand, and speaks of them as 'what God is doing'. This model of church is defended as a return to the experiences of Pentecost (Acts 2) and is held up as a God-given template for a passionate church in any period of history.

There is no doubt that authentic times of revival can be dramatic and life-changing for those involved and can impact a wide number of people. There is also no doubt that a desire for intimacy with God, the experience of the power of God and a yearning to draw many others to God should be central for all Christians. But the particular model offered by revivalism (the belief that revival will solve all the problems of the church) is a dubious blueprint.

For a start, revivalism is not a sustainable model. Revival is similar to the initial phase of a romance when a lover is besotted: it is a wonderful, giddy feeling while it lasts, but it cannot last for long. Studies by relationships experts indicate that the initial romantic fizz between two people lasts a maximum of a couple of years. After that it must settle down to a calmer, more everyday type of love and commitment. This is a vital shift if the love is to continue over the long haul. In any case, it would be unsustainable to remain at such a pitch of emotional intensity. A similar timescale seems to apply to revivals. Those Christians who pray and call for a permanent state of revival are like lovers who expect their love to remain at the fever pitch of the early days, and the results are sadly similar. People move from one partner (or church) to the next, in search of a promise of the elusive high, or else disillusionment sets in and people end up feeling betrayed and angry at being misled. Revivalism leaves many broken hearts in its wake.

Revivalism also encourages faddism. It cherishes a vision of mass conversion across a nation and fuels the hope that it is just around the corner. This in turn encourages a belief that we can hasten revival if only we find the right catalyst. Recent decades have seen the rise and fall of trends such as power evangelism, marching for Jesus, 'strategic level prayer warfare' against demonic principalities and powers, 'treasure-hunting' prayer for healing on the streets, the Toronto, Pensacola and Lakeland Blessings, and a wide range of other movements. Each one may well have contained many aspects that were good and beneficial. Taken together over a longer period of time, however, a wider pattern of faddishness has unfolded, with each new manifestation being first heralded as the key that will unlock the promised revival, and then forgotten when the next fad appears over the horizon.[3] The whole exhausting cycle of being told to prepare for a revival that never quite arrives has left many charismatics burnt out and disilllusioned, with many beating a path to calmer, more liturgical churches or leaving the faith altogether.

Added to this is the fact that revivalism, like a Motorhead concert, can deaden people's ears to subtler tones. In revivalist churches, an ecstatic style of worship and an expectation of the sensational and miraculous become the norm. The 'work of God' becomes identified with what goes on in large meetings. Sacramental, low-key or less visible expressions of faith can pale in comparison— receiving Holy Communion, care for the elderly, environmental projects, studying theology, befriending a neighbour, weeding the churchyard, helping move the chairs or doing the washing-up, developing an artistic project to God's glory, helping in the crèche, holding on to God when times are hard and healing miracles seem few on the ground. In fact, most of what the New Testament and church history would see as the normal Christian life tends to be marginalised and undervalued in the fervour of revivalism.

The Amos-Driven Church

This kind of church focuses on social justice to the exclusion of all else, and is named after the Hebrew prophet who called so passionately for justice. It gets fired up on issues such as human rights, poverty and environmental degradation, and offers a positive and helpful corrective to those types of church that have marginalised the social and cultural implications of the faith. But the risk in Amos-Driven Churches is that other core aspects of historic Christianity are seen as subservient to social activism. Biblically, the call to redeem societies and unjust structures cannot be separated from the call to personal discipleship and holiness. The call for justice is imperative, but it cannot be allowed to squeeze out essential aspects of the faith such as conversion, prayer, worship and the exploration of spiritual gifts. The activist version of the faith can end up every bit as partial and limited as the pietistic, inward-looking version.

To summarise our point so far in this chapter: some leaders in the church follow the likes of Hybels and Maxwell in adopting an overt model of top-down vision from business, and develop a specific vision for their own church. Others may shy away from the terminology of vision or may be unaware of it, yet they still have a very definite blueprint in mind for the future of their church. Either way, what results is the same: the destination is fixed. Shorter-term goals are set with a clear destination in view.

This is obviously a very different picture from that painted by the Spanish poet Machado, cited at the start of this book, which is an image of exploration and journey, of making the road as we walk. Throughout this book we have been sympathetic towards the open-endedness and provisionality expressed in Machado's poem, suggesting that it is a helpful model for church leadership. But does this imply ditching 'vision' from the Christian leadership vocabulary altogether? Might there be a way of exercising a purposeful and strategic ministry that does not suffer from the limitations of a top-down, fixed-destination, CEO model of leadership? We need to take a closer look at this kind of visionary model and its flaws.

Losing our vision

Many leaders cite famous words from the book of Proverbs as a basis for visionary leadership: 'Where there is no vision, the people perish' (Proverbs 29:18, KJV). It is significant, however, that these words have to be quoted from the King James Bible, which here misrepresents the Hebrew original. In reality, the original proverb contains no pointer towards today's management-style vision: it is concerned to contrast human anarchy with divine guidance. Newer and more accurate translations render the verse 'Where there is no revelation, people cast off restraint; but blessed are those who heed wisdom's instruction' (TNIV) or 'Where there is no prophecy, the people cast off restraint, but happy are those who keep the law' (NRSV).

A single misquoted verse hardly seems a good biblical foundation for an entire model of ministry. Serious questions are now being asked about this model in the business world, and questions must be asked about whether it ever was the best model for Christian leadership. First, though, we must consider the challenges from business.

1) **The world is changing.** The global financial crisis that began in 2007 sent shockwaves through not only the world of economics but also leadership theory. More accurately, the credit crunch became the most visible of a number of seismic shifts demonstrating that our world is changing fast and many of the old rules seem no longer to apply. Business theorists are increasingly using the same language as the new wave of missional church leaders, saying that the old maps are redundant.[4] Whatever the vision of the future we come up with, the one thing we can predict with certainty is that it is likely to be wrong. Missional church consultant Will Mancini comments, 'We can't extrapolate the present reality as we used to. The ten-year plan becomes an exercise in fantasy, not vision.'[5]

British management writer Jo Owen identifies three historic waves of leadership theory. 'Pre-Modern' approaches depended on traditions that were handed down from master to apprentice and carefully supervised by craft guilds. 'Modern' management was shaped by the culture of the 17th- and 18th-century Enlightenment, with its love of science, reason and universal laws. It worked on the assumption that the world was more or less predictable and that universal strategies would work equally well in any setting. Thirdly, Owen describes our current condition as a 'New World Disorder'. Old certainties are being questioned and discarded, many of the apparently successful organisations of the past are now struggling for survival, and the models on which they were built are being discarded or seriously questioned.

Owen notes that even the most persuasive accounts of the 'laws' for successful business and leadership, such as Jim Collins' *Good to Great*,[6] have proved short-lived and questionable. In his 2001 book, Collins identified eleven companies that his research team believed exemplified some enduring principles of true greatness. With the benefit of hindsight, Collins' conclusions seem rather more shaky. Among his eleven 'great' companies, by the end of that same decade Circuit City had gone bust, Gillette had been taken over, Fannie Mae had had to be bailed out by the taxpayer and Nucor had received a profit warning.

Long-term strategic vision setting made sense in a world where the future seemed relatively certain, where the world in which a business or church operated was predictable, and where most people accepted that there were established laws of success and growth on which strategy could be based. Owen concludes that today's leaders have to avoid the simplistic formulae of the past and must question orthodoxy. Survival and success, he says, now depend on our organisations being 'different in a relevant way'.[7] In other words, leaders need the courage to step out of line and begin to shape a unique and creative organisation.

2) **It was a flawed model of vision anyway.** A top-down, vision-and-goals model assumes that it is possible to envisage a solution from the start and set up goals to help move people towards a desired outcome. But what if that is not how vision setting or problem solving actually works? What if we only begin to understand a problem as we begin to tackle it? What if good leadership decision making is inescapably experimental, the art of adapting as new information becomes available? What if the people and places we encounter along the journey help to determine where we want to end up?

This is the claim of the stimulating book *Obliquity*, by economist and Financial Times columnist John Kay. Kay argues that objectives are best approached obliquely rather than directly, because the direct approach always tends to oversimplify and mislead. He points out that ultimate objectives are always so complex as to defy precise analysis or calculation: 'Decision making cannot proceed by defining objectives, analysing them into goals and subsequently breaking them down into actions. No priest or politician, counsellor or manager has the capacity to do this—and those who claim to, like Le Corbusier or Lenin, have an immense capacity to damage the complex systems they attempt to plan.'[8]

It may seem a little harsh to compare leading a small business or local church to the project of modernist architecture or running the Soviet Union. But Kay's claim is that similar principles do apply and that any leader who claims to have a clear vision of a final outcome that takes all factors into account is deluding himself and misleading others. Kay notes that a computer is good at solving a problem that we have specified and asked it to solve, 'but less useful when we are not quite sure what the problem is'.[9] How sure can a leader be that the final destination she has in mind is the best one for all concerned, one that takes every variable into account? Kay argues that, at the start of the process, she cannot. The course of the journey itself determines the destination.

Both of these points surely apply to church leadership today. Like businesses, we operate in a world of rapid change, where the context of our ministry is in constant flux; and church leaders are not immune from the practical issues highlighted by John Kay. God may be omniscient but even our clearest vision will be, at best, provisional and fallible. A vision that takes account of all possible eventualities and outcomes will always elude even the most skilled leader as we start out on a journey. In practice, we discover our destination as we go; we make a road as we walk. To this must be added some other specifically Christian considerations.

1) The visions we come up with are rarely broad enough. To pin down vision for a church risks singling out one aspect of church and emphasising it to the exclusion of others. The examples of church blueprints outlined earlier in this chapter are not so much wrong as partial: each one grasps an aspect of the faith (spiritual renewal, social justice, sound teaching, and so on). A vision needs

a visionary, and the vision will inevitably be determined by what the visionary can see in his mind's eye, which is in turn shaped by his own preferences and experiences, even his ambitions. But the faith of which we are custodians in our generation is much greater than any of these partial emphases.

2) **The visionary model risks excluding other wisdom.** Good vision-casting in a church context, according to its advocates, involves prayer and a process of discernment, and good visionary leaders involve others in their decisions. This focus on prayer and consultation is obviously a good thing, and there are clearly healthier, consultative versions of visionary leadership than the crude top-down version we have outlined so far. It remains nevertheless true that any vision process, by definition, involves 'seeing' a blueprint of a better future and fixing this vision in the mind of the leader, the leadership team and the congregation. Even the best vision has to be essentially static, set in stone for a period of time. This carries the risk that a visionary leader may be telling the people (even telling God) precisely what the local church needs and turning a blind eye to any pointers in other directions, or to wisdom that appears not to fit the vision.

Similarly, there is an inbuilt risk with a top-down model of vision that the focus of teaching and prayer in the church may become co-opted in the service of the vision, rather than being allowed to speak for itself and communicate a broader or even contradictory message. This can apply to the choice of Bible readings, the content of sermons, the focus of intercessions, the study material distributed to home groups, and so on. There is a risk that the vision of even the wisest leader subtly reshapes the gospel message that people hear in that church, or that the vision-driven church ends up offering only a partial gospel.

3) **People matter more than the destination.** Because most vision-casting comes from a leader or group of leaders, the leaders need to communicate the vision to the rest of the congregation and get them to 'buy in' to it. So a church driven by a vision inevitably

risks making the people fit the project rather than vice versa. Missional theologian Alan Roxburgh notes:

When we universalise a method like strategic planning, a method of achieving preset goals and objectives, we essentially turn every variable in the process, including human beings, into objects to be used in the achievement of a goal. There is no way around this. Strategic planning uses objectification to achieve ends... There can never be a justification for turning any human being into an object of someone else's goals and vision in the social community formed by the Spirit of God.[10]

An important biblical principle is that every person is made in the image of God, is infinitely precious, and has something unique to contribute to the church, as in Paul's image of the body with many parts in 1 Corinthians 12. The 20th century was littered with grand schemes, such as the slum clearance in many of Britain's cities, which put architects' visions before people and communities. For Christians, there has to be a better way, which values people more than even the best plans and programmes. The Christian faith is less about what I achieve and more about the values that motivate me as I go, and the way I treat others.

When I was young, there was no such thing as a hard-drive TV recorder, DVD recorder or even video recorder; we had to balance a cassette recorder on a stool close to the TV to capture something of a favourite TV programme. Some time ago, we rediscovered some audio cassettes that my wife had recorded, more than 30 years previously, of TV shows from her childhood, including 'Little House on the Prairie'. Her sister was so little at the time that she couldn't say 'Little House on the Prairie'. Instead what came out was 'House of the Fairy'. When we listened to one of the cassettes, recorded all those years ago, what we heard was a muffled recording of 'Little House on the Prairie' and, over it all, a high-pitched repetition of the words 'House of the Fairy'. Then there was another voice, that of a big sister getting furious with her little sister for ruining her recording. But my wife's sense of what was valuable on that recording has changed over the years. At the time, the only thing that mattered was the TV show; now the only important thing on the cassette is the reminder of a now grown-up person, a cherished relationship.

James Houston, Christian author and founder of Regent College, Vancouver, once suggested at a conference of church leaders that the minister's CV is written across the face of his or her spouse. This was met with a stunned silence from his audience, who were expecting a series of success tips for visionary leaders. But Houston was highlighting a vital Christian insight into success and achievement: the destination matters less than the relationships we form as we travel. The way I relate to people day-to-day makes a more eloquent statement than any number of vision statements and dynamic church programmes. When vision trumps kindness, something has gone seriously wrong in my ministry.

4) The journey matters as much as the arriving. Maybe we should see ministry not so much in terms of reaching a final destination in the shortest time possible, but as being about the things we see and learn along the way. The American architect Frank Lloyd Wright is famous for designing many prominent buildings, including the Guggenheim Museum in New York. In later life he recalled how, as a boy of nine, he had once walked with his uncle across a snowy field. His uncle was a driven and impatient man. Once they had walked across the field, the uncle turned round and pointed to the different tracks they had made. The uncle's footprints were precise and went in a perfectly straight line. Young Frank's tracks wandered and shuffled all over the place and sometimes backtracked on themselves. The uncle pointed out how his steps were goal-driven and direct, whereas the boy's wandered from the fence to the cattle to the woods and back again. In adulthood, Frank Lloyd Wright used to retell the story and add, 'I determined right then not to miss most things in life, as my uncle had.' Here is another vital Christian insight into success and achievement: the way we travel,

and the experiences we have along the way, matter as much as getting to our destination.

There is a related critique of the vision-and-goals model of ministry that is slightly harder to explain, but will make most sense at a gut level to those who value the Christian liturgical calendar (with its cycle of festivals and colours), and those who live and minister in rural settings.

A classic visionary model of strategic change, drawn from business, imposes its own structure on an organisation. In a sense, the fulfilment of the vision becomes the journey. Time is implicitly understood to move in a straight line, from the present moment to the envisioned ideal future state, and is divided up into interim goals. It sees time, in other words, as linear and progressive. On the other hand, the traditional Christian year moves cyclically. It enters into the key moments and moods of the gospel story in a rhythmic annual rotation. In the same way, rural life tends to be shaped more profoundly around the cycle of the seasons than does urban or suburban life. A liturgical or rural way of experiencing time as cyclical will be, at a deep level, in some tension with a no-nonsense, linear, visionary concept of time.[11]

Late 20th-century modernity (secular and spiritual alike) had an easy way of resolving the tension: it saw the one understanding of time as old-fashioned and primitive, the other as progressive and dynamic. A linear, visionary model of progress was enthusiastically seized on by church leaders frustrated by the slowness of the traditional, cyclical, 'Groundhog Day' ministry. With the benefit of hindsight, we need to ask whether something was lost in the process of shaping the church around the model of strategic business planning. We need to ask whether the traditional cycle of the Christian year and the turning of the seasons might, in fact, have been close to the bones of what it is to be human, to be embodied, to be Christian. The vital insight of the liturgical and rural approach to time is that, maybe, life moves most naturally in a spiral: ultimately heading somewhere but moving in a cyclical rather than a linear and goal-driven way, taking the scenic rather than the shortest route.

Where there is no vision...

Do we have to abandon the whole idea of goals, vision and planning in our churches? Is the only alternative to the business world's vision model a genial, unfocused chaos, in which nobody in a local church is sure where they are going and the aim is simply to do what we have always done? Do lazy and unmotivated clergy now have an excuse to do nothing purposeful at all? Heaven forbid! It is important, however, that we choose our metaphors wisely, because our metaphors shape our journeys and outcomes. There are good reasons to believe that the metaphor of vision is too static and inflexible, may not fit the realities of complex decision-making, is limiting, and undervalues the eccentric and unpredictable (including people), not to mention undervaluing the natural rhythms of the seasons and the Christian year. We have good reasons to search for a better image.

Rather than vision, a more helpful approach might draw on images such as 'pilgrimage' or 'quest'. These ideas carry a sense of journeying in a purposeful way, but they put the focus as much on the travelling as on the destination. They also carry overtones of excitement, discovery and risk.

Perhaps the most helpful metaphor, though, is that of being sent out on a *mission*. Like adventure or quest, it carries a sense of travelling purposefully: there is a definite reason for the journey but it does not put all the weight on the final destination. It also carries helpful overtones of excitement, discovery and risk.

Every episode in the original series of 'Star Trek' famously opens with the words, 'Space... the final frontier. These are the voyages of the starship *Enterprise*. Its five-year mission: to explore strange new worlds; to seek out new life and new civilisations; to boldly go where no man has gone before.' This is mission as exploration, mission as relational encounter. Captain James T. Kirk's five-year mission of exploration seems a better analogy for Christian leadership than the five-year vision of the European Salt Industry, released to an expectant public around the time when most of this chapter was being written (along with its targets for communicating with consumers about healthy eating). Mission also has an added emphasis on the urgency of the task: when James Bond is sent out on a mission, the fate of the world is always at stake.

The metaphor of mission has the added value of a long Christian heritage, which has not been totally discredited by the mistakes and abuses from the history of Christian missions. It also carries a theological emphasis that is absent from vision. The word 'mission' is derived from a Latin verb meaning 'to send'. We produce a vision, but we are sent out on a mission. More accurately, we are called to participate in the *missio dei*, the mission of God in the world.

Our shared mission

Is every leader called to find a unique mission for their church? I suggest that that would be a misunderstanding. There is only one big mission, but it will be earthed in very different settings, and each local church will have different windows on it, so there is no risk of homogeneity or blandness. What is this big mission? One thing is certain: whatever we identify as the overarching mission for all churches will need to be biblically rooted and big enough to encompass every dimension of God's call to his Church.

There is just such a core mission that comes direct from the teaching of Jesus and addresses questions of ultimate destination. Jesus says, '*Seek* his [God's] *kingdom*, and all these things will be given to you as well' (Luke 12:31; Matthew 6:33, my emphases). These words are the closest Jesus comes to offering a 'vision' for believers and leaders in the modern sense: he uses a metaphor of vision, the Greek verb *zeteo*, meaning to search or look for something. But this is no monolithic or blueprint vision.

The theme of the kingdom of God was the central focus of Jesus' teaching, particularly his parables. It appears 32 times in Luke's Gospel alone. In Mark's Gospel, Jesus' first recorded words are programmatic for his ministry: 'The time has come... The kingdom of God has come near' (1:15). The first request in the prayer Jesus taught his followers is 'Your kingdom come... on earth as it is in heaven' (Matthew 6:10). In Matthew's Gospel, a parallel but equivalent phrase is generally used—'the kingdom of heaven'— since Matthew was writing to Jews, and in Jewish usage 'heaven' or a similar term was often used in place of the name of God. But Matthew's phrase does not imply that the kingdom is located away from the earth: the kingdom is always earthly. The phrase always means the kingship or rule of God here on earth, 'divine government'.[12] Jesus teaches his followers to pray that the rule of God will be a reality on earth as it already is in heaven. While Paul was under house arrest in Rome at the end of his life, the kingdom of God was similarly the theme of his message to all who would listen (Acts 28:23, 31).

The kingdom of God describes a state of harmony between people and God, between people and people, and between people and the planet. There are glimpses of this in the Old and New Testaments alike: the kingdom is pictured as a new heaven and a new earth, creation restored, a time of homecoming and abundance where radical *shalom* is evidenced by the wolf and the lamb feeding together (Isaiah 65:17–25; Revelation 21:1). This was a normal expectation of the Judaism of Jesus' day—that there would one day be a 'day of the Lord', when the rule of God would be established in an apocalyptic culmination of history. But Jesus shows in his parables that the kingdom is arriving in quiet, unspectacular and everyday ways. He uses homely, down-to-earth images for the kingdom: it is as small as a grain of mustard seed, a tiny lump of yeast in a bowl of dough (Luke 13:18–21).

Our mission, says Jesus, is to pray and work for the coming of the kingdom of God, to collaborate with God in planting a small seed that will eventually grow to be a huge tree, and mixing in the small yeast that will one day leaven the whole lump of dough. One day the rule of God will be an eschatological reality over the whole earth. For now, we are to pray and work to see the kingdom come in our own day. This is a mission which encompasses all that is best in our partial models of church, including the need for conversion, the value of good worship and teaching, the power and gifts of the Holy Spirit, ethical living, evangelism and social justice. It is a holistic vision that avoids the stale sacred–secular divisions and body–soul dualisms that have so often plagued Christian reflection. It is a vision not of rescue from the earth but of the earth restored and renewed; it is a vision not of life reduced but life in all its fullness. It includes coming to faith, taking steps toward personal wholeness, care for the environment, relationships restored, using our God-given creativity, and so much more.

What the coming of the kingdom looks like in practice will vary from place to place, and this is part of the task of the local church leader. Our role is to help different people experience the coming of the kingdom of God in their everyday lives, in an astonishing range of ways. So it is right for each local church to set its own local priorities as it contributes towards an overarching kingdom mission. We participate in one big mission, but it is the privilege of each local church to discern how it can make its own unique contribution to the coming of the kingdom in its own locality.

Think mission rather than vision

On the 'mission' model, the prayer of the local church leader should be 'Your kingdom come, in this place and among these people', and this underlines the importance of the eight-way attentiveness outlined in Chapter 4. It is about paying attention to the local context, to the history and resources of the local Christian community and those places where the Spirit is already at work. As part of this attentiveness, there are some simple exercises a church can undertake to identify its own distinctives and mission priorities.

At this stage, it may be helpful to underline again the essential difference between vision and mission. Vision is an aspirational image of the future. It offers a snapshot of where we want to end up in a few years' time, and the steps we think we need to take to get there. It needs to be revisited approximately every three or five years. Mission, on the other hand, simply defines our purpose and reason for existence: who we are and what we are called to do. The claim of this chapter is that mission is generally a more helpful category for church leadership than vision.

In my experience, just about the least useful exercise for a church is hammering out a vision statement a paragraph long (as sometimes recommended by business and management consultants). In one of my churches, we spent an age working on just such a vision statement, only to put it in a drawer and never refer to it again. One reason was that the world had a nasty habit of changing around us and, in any case, it was almost impossible to predict exactly where we wanted to end up as a church. There were simply too many variables and imponderables. The other reason it ended up forgotten in a drawer was its length: our vision statement was far too long. It was unusable on letterheads or below the name of the church on our website, it could never be dropped quickly into sermons and nobody could remember it. Far more helpful was what I called our mission headline.

Shaping our mission headline

A mission headline (or strapline) is a short memorable phrase that identifies a brand, company or church. It has a dual focus of reminding existing members what the main distinctive of their church is and giving outsiders some sort of feel for what to expect if they join us. The ideal mission headline should be no more than six words long, preferably well under six. It should avoid characteristics that ought to define all churches—it is about identifying what is distinctive or special about us—and it should avoid the kind of jargon or clichés that might sound offputting to non-members.

This should not be a 'top-down' exercise in which a leader or leadership team imposes a strapline to which the rest of the church are expected to conform. That will simply generate resentment, and the gap between ideal and reality will quickly become apparent. Nor should the process be rushed. I have found that a good starting point for this exercise is an away-day or away-morning for the leadership of the church (in our case, the Parochial Church Council or PCC). With the help of a flipchart we discussed a range of questions, such as:

- If a guest visited our church several times and was asked 'What did you like best?' what might they say?
- If you were inviting a friend to our church for the first time, what one thing would you promise they would find there?
- Who comes to our church?
- What is our church's most significant contribution to its local area?
- What kind of atmosphere do we want people to find at our church?
- If you could choose a new name for your church—any name—what would it be, and why?
- If our church were an animal, what would it be, and why?

As we noted our answers, a relatively small number of key themes began to emerge. By the end of the session, we began to throw out our preliminary ideas for possible headlines and came up with a shortlist. We then took the shortlist away to mull over for a few weeks and shared our discussions with other church members. We also discussed our themes and preliminary ideas with a church member who worked in marketing, so had a good ear for the 'mood music' of our various suggestions. More suggestions emerged and a final list was distributed to the PCC in time for another discussion at the next meeting. By this stage, two headlines had emerged as favourites and it was a simple matter of voting on which we liked best.

The headline we agreed in one of my churches was 'Loving God, loving people', which neatly encapsulated Jesus' summary of God's own priorities (Mark 12:28–34) but also sent out a message to local people yearning for community, belonging and relationships, that they would find these in our church. We also liked the ambiguity in the fact that 'loving' could be a verb ('our aim is to love God and other people') or an adjective ('we aim to be a loving group of people and we have faith in a loving God').

In another of my churches, we chose 'Life in all its fullness'. This again encapsulated a key theme of Jesus (John 10:10) while also sending out a positive, engaging message to our local community: what they would find at our church was not irrelevant to real life but would help them find what life is really all about. We also liked it because it hinted at the 'feel' of our services. This was an inner-city church with a mix of people from different backgrounds and an exuberant style of worship. We wanted to suggest this feeling, but without using terms that sounded either cheesy or super-spiritual to outsiders, or as if they had come from a local council diversity policy document.

Other current mission headlines I particularly like, because they offer an engaging cameo of the church or organisation, include:

- Bath Abbey: Where heaven and earth meet
- St Mary's Bryanston Square: Non-drowsy
- Christian Aid: We believe in life before death
- St John's College, Nottingham: Creative Christian learning

Part of the skill of identifying a suitable mission headline is in finding the right balance of honesty and aspiration. We want to be honest about who we are as a church, but also to aim high and communicate something dynamic and appealing to our community. If we apply honesty alone, many of our churches might end up with a headline along the lines of:

- St John's Church: Mustn't grumble
- Puddlehampton Baptist Church: We don't like change

At the same time, a headline that is only aspirational risks setting up expectations that we cannot fulfil.

Shaping our mission priorities

Another valuable exercise can be shaping some memorable mission priorities. The aim is to come up with a list of five or six key areas that we as a church think are essential to our mission to our community. To repeat: our big mission is to work towards the kingdom of God becoming a reality, which I have suggested is the big mission for all churches given by Jesus himself. But the contexts in which each church carries out this mission vary enormously, so the kingdom coming in our own community might involve a special focus on elderly people, students, farmers, artists, street drinkers or young families with toddlers. Our ministry to that community might involve a particular focus on friendship over a cup of coffee, recovery groups, money advice, relationships counselling, hospital visiting or shared activities such as sport or rambling. The ways we worship God in church may be characterised by energy and excitement, space for quiet reflection, experimentation and creativity, or songs and music that are traditional and familiar to a particular section of the local community.

An exercise in mission priorities can help us clarify what we believe we as a church are called to do, out of all the things we could be doing. It can also help us know when to say 'no' to certain things. Churches are most effective when they do a few things well,[13] rather than spreading themselves thinly and doing nothing very well. An exercise in shaping mission priorities is probably best done with a representative group from the church, such as a Church Council. However, it is unrealistic to expect to hammer out both a mission headline and a set of mission priorities on the same occasion. My suggestion would be to keep the two away-days at least several months apart. At an away-day, questions to ask might include:

- What do we already do well?
- 'If we don't do x, we might as well shut down the church.' What is x for you?
- What would you love our church to become famous for?
- If you didn't go to our church, which church would you go to and why?
- Who are the main groups of people in our community?
- What are the felt needs of people in our community? Which of these needs do we currently engage with? Which do we not touch at all?

A provisional list of mission priorities can be drawn up and discussed with the rest of the congregation, through presentations in Sunday services, home groups, parent and toddler groups and the like, and a final list of mission priorities agreed. These priorities can then be displayed prominently on a noticeboard, on the church website and in other key locations where they will be seen, as well as being referred to regularly in talks.

Shaping our mission values

Some churches find it helpful to agree a few mission values, too. Mission values are not so much about what we do as how we aim to do it. They might include honesty, keeping a sense of humour, valuing diversity and, where there are disagreements, talking directly to the person concerned. The real test, of course, is that shaping mission values must become more than a paper exercise. The challenge is for us to live the values we claim to profess. The values statement of the US energy company Enron included a commitment to 'respect, integrity, communication, excellence'. Enron famously collapsed in 2001 amid a scandal involving corporate fraud and widespread internal corruption.

Missional DNA

This model of shaping a mission headline, mission priorities and mission values is only one suggestion. There are other approaches. Missional church consultants Roxburgh and Boren suggest a process that begins with listening to our own church members' life stories, concerns, interests and struggles to cope in a world that is changing rapidly. They emphasise the importance of creating 'safe spaces' where people know they are being listened to and their experiences are being taken seriously.[14] This might include setting up 'listening teams' of laity who can ask questions such as:

- Reflect back on your entire experience at our church. When did you feel most engaged, alive and motivated? What was happening that contributed to that experience?
- What do you think are the most important, life-giving characteristics of our church?
- When are we at our best?
- Describe a time in our church when God was most real and alive for you.[15]

The listening process can also happen in weekend workshops that address particular issues of change in society, where people are invited to tell their own stories and share their own struggles, as well as in traditional pastoral care encounters.

The findings from this listening process can be read with a view to spotting recurring themes and metaphors, in addition to asking where God appears to be in people's answers and what signs of hope can be discerned. The next step they suggest is a number of feedback seminars, or invitations to further dialogue, that ask what next steps the church might make on the basis of what has been heard. A fundamental conviction of Roxburgh and Boren is that 'the job of the leadership is not to come up with grand plans for the congregation but to cultivate an environment in which the missional imagination of the people of God is called forth'.[16] In time, the church together can enter an 'experimental stage' where people are given permission to try fresh experiments in living and worshipping together that address some of the issues that emerged from the process of listening and dialogue. These are likely to be experiments in reconnecting with people in our local communities and involving the practice of hospitality.

Richard Impey, parish development adviser for Sheffield Diocese, suggests a similar process of listening for a local church, which he describes as 'working with the wisdom of the congregation'.[17] All these models for listening and consultation are nothing more than suggestions. It may well be that you can devise a much better model of your own. Whatever process we engage in, the underlying point is this: it has to be about discerning the DNA of our own local church and community, discovering what it is that makes us unique.

Treasure in an unpromising field

All of this is not to deny that there are times when a minister has to take on a more proactive role. There is a vital place for the inspirational leader, with fresh ideas, who takes a lead and is required to make decisive and controversial decisions—particularly where a congregation is at a low ebb or dysfunctional, or where most church members are either new to faith or on the fringes of faith. A listening style of leadership does not preclude decisiveness, initiative and even confrontation.

At the same time, many clergy in struggling situations will be tempted to shake their heads in despair at the idea that their congregation is brimming full of latent wisdom and 'missional imagination'. But the underlying point made by Roxburgh, Boren and Impey remains true, even in the most unpromising settings. The best sort of leadership is not about importing or imposing, but loving and listening. For all its problems and limitations, the place where you find yourself is the place where you have been called to minister, with this particular group of people, at least for now. Sometimes the biggest adventure of leadership is discovering potential where little has hitherto been apparent.

Amateur metal detector enthusiast Terry Herbert lived alone and on state benefits. In July 2009 he was trudging around an ordinary-looking field in rural Staffordshire with his detector when he discovered something in the ground: a piece of gold. When excavated, the site turned out to contain the largest hoard of Anglo-Saxon gold ever discovered, three times the quantity found in the famous Sutton Hoo ship burial of 1939, plus a significant amount of silver. The hoard included more than 1500 pieces from around the year AD700, including weapons, helmets and Christian crosses. The gold finds included some stunning ornamentation from Anglo-Saxon swords, studded with gems and bearing tiny images of interlaced beasts.

Leadership is the art of looking for buried treasure. Who will discover the treasure hidden in the unpromising-looking fields of your neighbourhood if you are not there, patiently looking for it?

Snapshot: Miracle in Jersey

Ebenezer Methodist Church found it hard to look to the future with optimism. Its location may have been idyllic, as a rural community in the north of the island of Jersey, but its ageing congregation, drawn from the local farming community, had been in decline for many years. Then events on their doorstep confronted the small congregation with a stark choice. Would they continue in comfortable introspection and slow decline or grasp the nettle of change for the sake of mission to their local community?

In March 2007, it was announced that the neighbouring Highfield Hotel was to be sold and turned into apartments. One practical implication for Ebenezer's members was that they would lose their Sunday parking. For years, Ebenezer had had an informal arrangement with the hotel that worshippers could use its parking spaces during services. But there was a wider and more challenging implication, too: there would be a fresh influx of new people living next door to the church, including many young families. Would the congregation make any special effort to welcome these families, and would they rethink their pattern and style of services in order to help the newcomers genuinely to participate in the life and worship of their church?

The congregation realised that the hotel redevelopment might be a God-given opportunity to connect with a new generation of people in their local community. They entered into negotiation with the hotel developer and local landowners about the possibility of creating a new 50-space car park for the church. The developer was happy to work with them on this, but the existing church building would have to be modified to provide car access to the new parking area. This in turn opened up the option of a bigger scheme to reorder the church and hall for community as well as church use, and introduce a new pattern of services. It was a daunting prospect for a small community not used to rapid change—and the price tag for doing the job properly would be a staggering £400,000, hardly small change for a church of 40 people.

Ebenezer's minister, Billy Slatter, challenged the church that if this exciting but scary project were to happen, they would have to kick-start it by raising £60,000 in a single gift day. The small congregation prayed fervently for the money to enable the work to start. On the Sunday morning following the gift day, it was announced that £59,600 had been given. By the end of that same day, the full target amount had been raised. Within just one year, all the necessary permissions had been granted, contracts and legalities sorted out and the building work completed. Billy Slatter and the congregation of Ebenezer do not hesitate to describe the changes to their building and pattern of worship as a miracle.

In September 2008, a celebration service was held to open the new premises. The renovated building includes new toilets with baby-changing facilities, a fully equipped kitchen, a carpeted hall with a wet play area for messy children's activities, and a number of rooms available for local people to hire for parties and clubs, all with full access for disabled people. Today the refurbished hall at Ebenezer is so popular that the church has to refer bookings to other churches.

At the same time, the Ebenezer congregation decided to introduce a new service aimed at young families, after consulting with them about what they would find most helpful. The new service is just 30 minutes long. It has a café church format, which is informal and interactive, with families sitting at tables with drinks. The relaxed atmosphere means there is no embarrassment for parents if young children become noisy or restless.

The overhaul of Ebenezer Methodist Church has involved not only new premises but a fresh openness and relevance to their local community. Other churches in the same Methodist circuit have been so inspired by what Ebenezer has achieved that they are now starting schemes of their own.

7

Rethinking guidance

In search of guidance

In the last chapter we questioned whether a model of vision borrowed from business management is the best model for shaping a church. We suggested that a rather uncritical adoption of business models may have distorted the process of helping a church to a better future. But what if there is a deeper theological root to our problem? What if many Christians, and church leaders in particular, are operating with an inadequate and unhelpful model of divine guidance? Once again, this brings to the fore the question of whether we operate with a blueprint mentality or whether we believe that God entrusts us with the freedom to be creative and improvise. The underlying theological issue is whether God has everything planned in advance or whether he gives humans a significant level of freedom, and so, in effect, takes risks.[1]

The classic management approach to vision encourages a leader to have a clear, compelling vision of the future. In churches this might be expressed in terms of a vision of how the church will look in five or ten years' time, or a model of church that has been successful elsewhere. Theologically, it fits comfortably with the widespread idea that God already has a perfect plan in his mind, both for the shape and direction of my ministry and for my church. Leaders might speak in terms of 'discerning God's will for my life and ministry', 'discerning God's vision for our church' or 'being in the centre of God's will'. In other words, God himself has a blueprint vision in mind for my ministry and my church, and my job is to find out what it is.

But is it true that God has a 'plan' or a 'vision', which we need to discern and to which we need to conform? Might a more biblical model of guidance be that God metaphorically shrugs his shoulders and says, 'Doesn't bother me either way—you decide'? This is no academic debating point. It has direct bearing on a range of crucial questions faced by church leaders. How do I know if God is calling me to the ordained ministry in the first place? Am I currently in the right church or denomination? How do I know if it is time to move to a new church? Does God have a specific church in mind that I should move to? How do I discern and implement God's vision (if there is such a thing) for my church?

In this chapter we shall question the blueprint model of guidance assumed by many Christians and church leaders and explore a more creative alternative. A number of authors have written on this subject and raised serious questions about how biblical the traditional approach of many Christians to guidance really is.[2] Nevertheless, in my experience, most church leaders and congregations still offer it as the unquestioned biblical pattern, and it remains the only approach to guidance that many Christians have ever been taught or seen modelled by other believers. We shall need to explore some Bible passages in some detail in order to respond to the widely assumed biblical basis for the blueprint model.

Blueprint guidance

Here are a few scenarios involving people looking for guidance:

- A minister is unsure about whether to apply for a job in a different part of the country. He wants to follow God's perfect will for his life, so he prays earnestly for an inner voice or external signpost to make things clearer.

- A girl prays, 'If it's right for me to move to this new job, let me see a blue VW camper van in the next 24 hours.' She sees one and decides that God must want her to change job.
- A church prays earnestly about whether God wants them to plant a new congregation on a housing estate. They do not want to go ahead unless it is made clear to them that this is God's will.
- A recently retired woman is unsure how she can best use the time she now has available. She prays that God will reveal to her what he wants her to do.
- A man prays, 'Lord, if it's right for me to marry this girl, I pray that Manchester United will beat Tottenham tonight.' United lose, so he doesn't pop the question.
- A church council is unsure whether to embark on a costly re-development of the church hall complex. The church is divided on the matter and the council members appear to have reached a stalemate. During their meeting, the minister suggests that they all wait silently for inner promptings from the Holy Spirit to break the *impasse* and help them decide one way or the other.

For countless Christians, these various scenarios illustrate something of how guidance works. The majority view in many churches holds that God has a plan for the future direction of the ministry there, as well as for members' personal decisions, such as whom to marry, what job to take and how many children to have. God has a clear opinion on every choice we make and there is a right or wrong option according to the blueprint in God's mind.

If that is true, then guidance becomes defined as searching for God's very specific will in all the details of life. Prayer for guidance means asking God for signs and promptings that reveal the right course of action. Our responsibility is to find the one correct choice that God has in mind for us. In terms of church leadership, a primary role of the leader becomes to discover the hidden blueprint in the mind of God for her congregation. The main way she attempts to do this is by paying close attention to a combination of inner impressions and outward signs as she prays, and she will interpret circumstantial evidences, in the world around her and from other people, as signposts towards God's perfect outcome. In some circles, a life that attends devoutly to these inner impressions and outer signs is seen as an ideal model of Christian spirituality.

A number of recent publications assume this model of guidance. The popular author and megachurch pastor Charles Stanley applies it to all types of guidance. His book *God Has a Plan for Your Life* contains much that is helpful about how we can live obediently and wisely, but it is all based on one big assumption. Stanley explicitly states that the fact of God's sovereignty over the world necessarily means that he has a specific course he wants each of us to follow, and that there are right and wrong choices at every crossroads in our lives. So the reader is told, 'Instead of thinking, What about me and my desires?, the right question to ask is, "Lord, what is Your desire for my life? Please show me Your plan, and make Your will absolutely clear so I can do it."'[3] Stanley is confident that this is the only correct theological framework for guidance: 'There is no doubt that God has a plan for our lives, and He wants us to discover it and live in the middle of it.'[4] The back cover wording asks the prospective reader, 'Are you ready to take the first step to discover exactly what God has for you?' Those words 'discover' and 'exactly' speak volumes: they tell us that God has a specific blueprint in mind for each of us.

The same assumption is applied to the practicalities of leading a local church, in *Growing the Church in the Power of the Holy Spirit* by Brad Long, Paul Stokes and Cindy Strickler.[5] The central metaphor of the book is of a divine–human dance in which the Spirit takes the lead and it is up to the church leader to follow this lead. The authors see the image of the dance as a form of cooperation, but they are clear that 'we are called as coworkers sharing in the dynamic friendship and dominion with the King of the universe as he *implements his will* among us' (emphasis mine).[6] The deeper theological principle which is assumed, but never substantiated, is that the Spirit has a blueprint for my church and it is up to me as leader to cast off my 'merely human priorities'[7] and discern that perfect plan. The authors explicitly denigrate the use of 'our own wisdom, understanding, experience, and strength', because these are bound to be in opposition to God's agenda for our lives and the best outcomes for our church.[8]

But there are at least four good reasons to question this model of guidance.

It starts with the wrong question

Evangelical scholar Haddon Robinson provocatively suggests that when we ask the question, 'How can I know the will of God?' we may be asking a fundamentally pagan question. He cites the example of kings and generals in the ancient world who would consult oracles to find the guidance of the gods for their plans. The usually vague and enigmatic responses would then allow the person in search of guidance to read in their own preferences but to feel as if they had some sort of divine backing.[9] Instead, Robinson suggests that a more biblical question may be simply 'How do I make good decisions?'

It is strangely absent from the Bible

Given the popularity of the traditional blueprint model of guidance, it can come as a surprise to discover that it is nowhere to be found in the Bible. It is true that the scriptures do speak of God's will, but in two senses:

- **God's sovereign will:** The Bible indicates that God does have a 'big picture' will through history. He is the one 'who works out everything in conformity with the purpose of his will' (Ephesians 1:11). The atoning death of Jesus Christ was 'chosen before the creation of the world' (1 Peter 1:20). Even the circumstances of the trials and execution of Jesus happened according to 'God's deliberate plan and foreknowledge' (Acts 2:23). As the book of Revelation portrays so powerfully, God has big-picture purposes in history that will not be thwarted by either human or demonic agency.

- **God's moral will:** There is no shortage of passages in the New Testament about God's will. Paul writes that we should 'test and approve' God's 'good, pleasing and perfect will' (Romans 12:2), and should 'not be foolish but understand what the Lord's will is' (Ephesians 5:17). On closer inspection, however, such passages turn out to be about God's moral will for all believers—the broad parameters within which we should be living our lives. They are not about whether I should apply for this particular job, marry this particular person or plant a new church.

Perhaps the most popular verse cited in favour of the traditional view of divine guidance comes from the prophet Isaiah: 'Whether you turn to the right or to the left, your ears will hear a voice behind you, saying, "This is the way; walk in it"' (Isaiah 30:21). But if we read this passage in context, we find that the 'way' referred to is God's law. Faithfulness to God's law was often described in the Hebrew scriptures in terms of not turning to the right or left (see, for example, Joshua 1:7). Furthermore, the 'voice' referred to appears to be the voice of the wise human teacher mentioned in the previous verse, not the Spirit of God. This is a verse about the need to pay heed to godly teachers who help us walk in the path of God's moral will; it does not tell us that God has a blueprint in mind for our entire journey.

There are any number of biblical examples of God calling a person to a particular task at a particular time: think of Moses, Philip, Esther, for example. Such a call usually comes in the form of special guidance, which is unique to that person and situation and often involves a miraculous and unmistakable sign (such as a burning bush or an angel). But these instances of 'supernatural' leading arrive unbidden and unsought by the person receiving them. What we do not find anywhere in scripture is the idea that God has an individual will for each person or a plan for every decision of their life, and that believers should be looking to God to make their life-choices for them. That is true even for those biblical characters who receive direct and detailed guidance for a particular event or decision. Intriguingly, at no point do we ever overhear a biblical character saying that they were doing something because it was God's will for their life, or praying to find God's will for their life. The terminology of guidance used by so many Christians today is curiously absent from the pages of the Bible.

It results in anxiety

The traditional model of guidance tends to produce Christians who are anxious and worried that they may be deviating from God's perfect blueprint, his one-and-only will. How do I ever really know if I'm on track or not? If I fail to discern the will of God about my job, my relationship or my church, is it because he is not telling me or because I have not prayed enough about it, or because I have not been sufficiently attentive to the inner promptings or external signs?

Added to this is the anxiety that I may miss altogether the blueprint that God has in mind but I have failed to discern. Will God then be permanently disappointed in me? Will I end up with a second-best life? The picture of God that emerges from this model risks being that of an inscrutable micro-manager who has my ideal life planned down to the tiniest detail but refuses to share most of the information with me. At best, he may give me a warm fuzzy feeling, a dream or a series of coincidences to point me in the right direction. How do I then interpret obstacles to what seems like the right path? Are they signs from God that I am embarking on the wrong course of action? Or are they tests of faith, hurdles to be jumped over?

This is not a terribly appealing picture of God, and it is hard to square it with the picture of God in the scriptures. It bears little relation to Jesus' portrait of God as a loving Father in the story of the prodigal son, and it seems at odds with Paul's confidence that 'in all things God works for the good of those who love him' (Romans 8:28). These biblical passages suggest a very different picture of how God operates.

It encourages passivity and immaturity

The scriptures encourage us to grow into maturity and godliness, to learn discernment. They reveal, time after time, that God invites our collaboration with his purposes for the world, by prayer and action. He wants mature people who love, act, communicate and take initiatives. He gives us freedom and responsibility. This is at odds with the traditional model of guidance, which effectively takes the responsibility for choosing and acting out of my hands. All I can do is sit and wait until God reveals the next step. Some Christians become almost paralysed and feel unable to do anything significant in their lives without an explicit sign from God. Some effectively lose the ability to carry out decision-making over the longer term. It is a model that begins with a commendable desire to act in accordance with the will of God, but can end up fostering an inappropriate and unChristian passivity and immaturity.

The traditional model also tends to push our decisions beyond the criticism of others. It assumes that God has one perfect will for an area of my life, and, if I feel that my inner promptings or circumstantial signs have revealed this one perfect will to me (I must marry Sarah, become a plumber, move abroad, or adopt this radical new direction for my church), it is hard for others to challenge me. In the minds of young and immature believers, this can result in an unwarranted certainty or dogmatism about a course of action. It can also be true of immature or insecure church leaders in their 'God-given' vision for a church. Who would dare challenge the will of God? Another kind of example might be the Christian who claims that 'God gave her' this poem or that song. Others, more experienced in the writing of poetry or songs, might have valuable suggestions and improvements to make, but, if the poem or song is claimed to have been dropped fully formed from heaven, like the Qur'an or the Book of Mormon, that effectively silences questions and criticism and can seem to negate the need for hard work and craftsmanship. Good guidance, like good art, benefits from the broadest possible range of sources of creative input and refinement.

In reality, the tangent of biblical revelation moves away from detailed regulation of believers' lives towards greater freedom and responsibility. In Galatians 4, Paul uses the analogy of children and adults. The Old Testament laws were 'guardians and trustees' to keep God's people under close supervision (4:2) because they had the status of young children. Then, with the coming of Christ comes freedom and maturity. Christians, writes Paul in Galatians 5, are no longer under the Jewish law but, rather, have the indwelling Holy Spirit. The biblical tangent moves from external supervision and detailed instruction to an inner power and freedom to decide with wisdom and maturity. It moves from laws written on tablets of stone to values written in the heart.

Gideon's fleece

Despite these four question marks over the traditional approach to guidance, many Christian leaders continue to assume its truth and teach it to their congregations. Lurking at the back of their mind is a story from the Old Testament which appears to give it credence.

For some Christians, the decisive precedent that proves God has an individual blueprint plan for the lives of believers is the story of Gideon's fleece, as told in Judges 6:36–40. God calls Gideon to lead the Israelite armies against their enemies, the Midianites, but Gideon is anxious and tells God that he needs an unequivocal sign to prove that the attack really is his will. He puts out a woollen fleece on the threshing-floor where people thresh the grain at harvest time. He then tells God that if God really wants him to deliver Israel as promised, in the morning he wants to find dew on the fleece, but the ground around it bone dry. This is precisely what happens, but Gideon is still unconvinced. He prays again, this time asking God for the opposite sign: for the fleece to be dry and the ground to be wet. Sure enough, that is what he finds.

Some see Gideon's fleece as a definitive model for divine guidance, revealing that God has a perfect individual plan for Gideon's life. They believe that Gideon's fleece is a normative way to find guidance at key points along life's journey. Such a believer might pray to God along the lines of one of our earlier examples: 'If it's right for me to change my job, let me see a blue VW camper van in the next 24 hours. That's my fleece.' But it is highly questionable that Gideon's fleece gives us any kind of model for divine guidance, for at least two reasons.

Firstly, Gideon is not asking for circumstantial evidence. He is not asking for normal circumstances to turn out in a certain way as a sign (such as a certain type of chariot happening to drive by). Gideon asks God for an out-and-out miracle, something that could not possibly happen by chance, because he wants to hear directly from God. If a leader today asks for everyday circumstances to turn out in a particular way and calls it a 'fleece', that is not the same as what Gideon did. In the Bible there are no examples of God guiding people through trivial circumstantial evidence. God appears not to be in the business of manipulating soccer games or forcing VW camper van drivers to drive by a different route, so that you and I can know whether to marry somebody, change our job or appoint a particular person as our new associate minister.

There is no doubt that God does give miraculous signs to particular individuals at key moments in salvation history, but it does not follow that he has a blueprint pattern for their whole life (there is no evidence, biblically, that he does). Nor does it follow that asking for miraculous signs is the normal way to receive guidance. Even in Bible times, these cases were rare exceptions. The normal pattern we are led to expect is the cultivation of wisdom in order to become the sort of person who makes good decisions, and the ability to weigh options carefully in a godly way.

A key biblical character such as King David appears never to have experienced a single miraculous sign by way of guidance. One of the characters who receives the most direct promptings from God is Paul, but even Paul's normal method of decision-making is to weigh up the options before him and make an informed decision. For example, he comments, '*If it seems advisable* for me to go also...' (1 Corinthians 16:4); elsewhere we are told that Paul '*decided* to go back through Macedonia' to avoid the Jews who were plotting against him (Acts 20:3), and that he '*had decided* to sail past Ephesus to avoid spending time in the province of Asia, for he was in a hurry to reach Jerusalem' (v. 16) (emphases mine).

The same pattern applies to the process of decision-making in the early church. The apostles find themselves over-stretched, so they choose Stephen and six others to take on the task of food distribution (Acts 6:3). At the Council of Jerusalem, the apostles decide that it would not be right to burden the Gentiles with endless rules, so, after discussion, they take a decision about which regulations are essential for Christians (15:1–21). Afterwards they decide who will go to Antioch with Paul and Barnabas (v. 22). Paul and Luke take a decision that they should remain in Athens and send Timothy to Thessalonica (1 Thessalonians 3:1–2). This is the normal pattern for decision-making in the early church. What we do not see is members praying time after time to know God's one-and-only will in each situation. A number of options might be equally viable, so they use their God-given wisdom to make a decision.

The second reason to question the model of Gideon's fleece

is that it was an expression of unbelief. God had already met with Gideon through an angelic messenger—or was it God in person? (Judges 6:11–16). Gideon had already seen meat and bread supernaturally consumed on a rock (vv. 19–22). He knew perfectly well what God had asked him to do. The story of the fleece is not a model for guidance for all time. Rather, it shows Gideon's lack of faith. The constant testing of God and asking for signs is not seen in the Bible as a good thing. Indeed, it is seen as Gideon's weakness. The Old Testament law condemns those who practise divination, attempting to foretell the future or peer into the unknown (Deuteronomy 18:10), and Jesus condemns people who are always looking for signs (Mark 8:11–12). Believers are not encouraged in the Bible to keep on asking for signs to settle their doubts. They are not encouraged to keep on asking God for the 'right' option at every crossroads. Rather, we are encouraged to cultivate wisdom and a renewed mind, and we are encouraged to be filled with the Spirit so that we are empowered to make right decisions. This is not to be written off as 'merely human' decision-making. Biblically, it is seen as the normal Christian approach to guidance.

A better model of guidance

We are not saying that God does not guide, or that we should never pray for guidance. What we are saying is that there are serious difficulties with a traditional blueprint model of guidance, and that there must be a better model which fits with scripture and will be more helpful to us as we look to make important decisions.

I would suggest that a more biblical model involves one principle and four pointers. The one principle is that God does not actually have any sort of 'plan' for my life (or my church, for that matter) at all. Far more exciting, he has a *purpose*: that I should live for his praise and glory (Ephesians 1:12, 14) and join in his cosmic plan to bring everything under the Lordship of Jesus (vv. 9–10). Within this broad framework, I have a huge amount of freedom. As we have already begun to explore in this chapter, the best sort of guidance for how I should exercise my God-given freedom is likely to come from the following areas.

First, God's sovereign will: We locate ourselves within God's big picture of human history, our own story finding its setting within God's grand narrative for the cosmos. We collaborate with the redemptive purposes of God the Father, through a faith commitment to Jesus Christ and by the indwelling presence of the Spirit. We collaborate with the mission of God to bring the good news of his kingdom to the ends of the earth.

Second, God's moral will: There is a huge amount of moral guidance from God in scripture, including the moral principles of the Mosaic law, the teachings of the Old Testament prophets (particularly their call to justice), the teachings of Jesus (particularly his insistence on love in action as being central to our moral vision), and the development of the Pauline fruit of the Spirit.

Third, wisdom: A large section of the Old Testament is known as wisdom literature, specifically the books of Proverbs, Job and Ecclesiastes, and the importance of wisdom is underlined in the New Testament (for example, James 1:5; 3:13–18). The word 'wisdom' is at the heart of Jewish and Christian spirituality, with its emphasis on relating our faith to the complexities of life in discerning and appropriate ways. The insights of wisdom, says Proverbs, are more precious than silver, gold or rubies; wisdom is built into the very structures of creation from the start (Proverbs 8), and so gives the basis for sound human decision-making. Solomon is commended for asking God for the gift of wisdom above all else, and his wisdom is repeatedly celebrated (1 Kings 3; 4:29–34; 10:23–24). Biblical wisdom is down-to-earth, rooted in the practical wisdom of the home, family and time-honoured tradition (Proverbs 2:1–2; 4:1–13), and deepened by observing the natural world (6:6–8) and learning from our mistakes (12:1). Ultimately, true wisdom is a gift of God (2:6).

This biblical theme of wisdom is closely related to Paul's idea of the 'renewing of our minds' (Romans 12:2), the ability to see things differently from other people, seeing things as God sees them. The person who cultivates wisdom and whose mind is being renewed makes wiser decisions when it comes to marriage or jobs. If a wise person thinks about a job option, he looks at more than just the salary. He looks at his motives for wanting the job, how it will affect his family life, whether it uses his God-given talents, whether other people think he would be good at the job, and so on. A wise person will look for the broadest possible range of criteria when decision-making, including the wisdom of others more mature than herself.

Fourth, the prompting of the Spirit: We have said that, biblically, the heart of guidance lies in cultivating wisdom and following broad principles, which we apply in our own context. Does this mean there is no role for inner promptings, circumstantial evidence or miraculous signs to guide us? These may happen, and it is wonderful when they do, but many advocates of the traditional view of guidance put the cart before the horse in this regard. They see these events as primary sources of God's guidance. In reality, the biblical precedent for them is thin compared to the clear biblical emphasis on God's sovereign will, his moral will and the need to develop wisdom. Inner impressions and circumstantial or miraculous signs may supplement these sources of guidance but must never supplant them.

Impressions and the interpretation of circumstances are highly subjective. We need to apply wisdom as we look to interpret the meaning of impressions and hunches, so that we do not put ourselves in the position of the army general from the ancient world who reads his own preferred outcomes into the words of an oracle. Most important of all, our focus must be on God rather than signs from God. We should love God for who he is, rather than for what he can do for us personally.

Having issued these *caveats*, we must not lose sight of the fact that, since the Day of Pentecost, God has given us not a tablet of laws but his own indwelling presence. Jesus tells his disciples that the invisible power and presence of God will come and make a home inside them: the Spirit will 'guide them into all the truth' (John 16:13). If we take biblical precedent seriously, we might expect the Spirit to give guidance for particular tasks at key times. This might happen through dreams and visions, by speaking directly to our heart or will, or in more dramatic ways. Sometimes the Spirit can guide by closing doors or saying 'no' to our prayers, or he might activate our conscience, so that we become more sensitised to right and wrong and are enabled to make wiser decisions. It is possible that the Spirit will be at work in a series of apparent 'coincidences', which seem to point us in a particular direction.

There is a range of ways in which the Spirit might guide. What we do not see in the scriptures, however, is the Spirit as oracle, giving instant, easy answers so that we do not have to consult the moral guidelines of the Bible or think for ourselves, and so that we do not have to grow in wisdom or consult others. A sound approach to guidance is more likely to involve the Spirit sensitising us to God's moral guidelines, helping us in our areas of moral weakness and equipping us to make wiser choices.

Vocation and calling

So often, we prefer to jump directly to fine details. Should we have another child? Should I join this group? Should we replace the church heating system? We look for instant, detailed guidance that makes our hard decisions for us, rather than working them through for ourselves from core principles that God has already given us. We say, 'God, tell me if I should marry Hannah.' But what if God does not mind who I marry, but instead gives principles to guide me? Perhaps his concern is not whether I marry Hannah or Helen but that I choose wisely, based on sound principles: my prospective partner and I need to be spiritually compatible, I need to love being in her company, and I need to trust her completely. We say, 'God, tell me if I should become a teacher or a minister or a plumber.' But perhaps God has no preference about what job I do and is happy for me to decide, asking the right questions to help me make a wise decision. What are the talents he has given me? What am I passionate about? What do other people tell me I am good at? What can I do that makes the world a better place?

Some may be concerned that this 'wisdom' model of guidance undermines the traditional idea of calling, particularly regarding a vocation to ordained ministry. The idea of vocation is generally assumed to mean that God has a blueprint for the minister's life, that he has already chosen the person he wants to be a pastor or missionary, and that this call is discerned in significant measure by the person sensing an inner prompting.

This raises some important questions, not least whether it is right to separate out a 'vocation' to ordained ministry or other full-time church work from other, more secular callings, as many churches have done over the years. Biblically, this is a hard distinction to sustain. One of the great insights of the Reformation, and the 17th-century Puritans in particular, was that God's 'cultural mandate' to humanity to be creative with the raw materials of the earth (Genesis 1:27–29) means that he calls people to the full range of occupations: teaching, farming, home-making, business, politics, volunteer work, and so on.[10] So whatever we conclude about vocation and calling, it needs to apply to all God's people. If we believe that God calls us to a specific occupation, this belief needs to apply equally to the journalist as to the pastor.

Many Christian thinkers do question whether God really does have a plan for our lives that involves a call to a specific occupation, as we have been doing in this chapter. One of the more thoughtful advocates of a 'wisdom' model of guidance, US theologian Garry

Friesen, explicitly questions a traditional model of call, whether to the ordained ministry or any other occupation.[11] He makes the case that, biblically, an explicit call from God, such as Paul's calling to be an apostle (Romans 1:1; 1 Corinthians 1:1), is a rare exception rather than the norm, and that at no point do we read in scripture of a 'call' being communicated through an inner impression. He notes that in neither Old nor New Testament is a specific call from God either promised or required before a person takes on an occupation, task or ministry, and there is no biblical instruction to seek out such a call.

Other Christian thinkers question Friesen's debunking of the traditional understanding of calling, pointing out that God does call people in the Bible to specialised ministries—for example, the craftspeople who work on the tabernacle (Exodus 31), prophets (Isaiah 6) and kings (1 Samuel 16). Jesus, also, clearly calls his disciples to their unique vocation (Luke 5). These thinkers follow the Puritans in believing that God does sovereignly call all people to particular occupations.

Even if we grant that God does call people to special tasks, and that this call might involve inner promptings of the Holy Spirit, we are given no sense that God wishes to micro-manage every detail of that call, or the rest of our lives. King David and the apostle Peter may have been called to special roles but there is no evidence that they looked to God for specific guidance at every turn, or believed that God had a detailed plan for every aspect of their life. Perhaps we should conclude with the late Cardinal Suenens of Belgium that God may not have a plan for my life, but he has a dream and a purpose for it.[12]

Freedom within boundaries

In 1843, the Danish philosopher Soren Kierkegaard noted in his journals the truism that life is lived forwards, but understood backwards. Yet human nature is such that we long for the reassurance of understanding life forwards, too. When this desire is combined with a theology of a sovereign God who knows the future and a Spirit who guides (both sound biblical principles in themselves), it is tempting to conclude that the truly spiritual person must be able to have privileged access to an infallible road map for the rest of the journey, or at least for the next stage in the journey. For all its popularity in today's church, however, this model of guidance seems to have little scriptural basis.

The biblical evidence points to an understanding of guidance that involves God giving us freedom within boundaries. We can enjoy our freedom to collaborate with God in making our own future, rather than getting stressed about whether we fit a blueprint that may not exist, even in the mind of God. What we are invited to is far more creative and exciting than constantly asking for signs. God gives us the freedom to work with him to create the future. Biblically, God does not appear to have any kind of plan for your life or my life, for your church or my church, just an ocean of possibilities. It is up to us to use our freedom wisely as we seek to shape a unique and creative church.

Snapshot: The Family Centre

St Christopher's, Springfield, is a Church of England parish church in a multi-faith and largely Muslim area of south-east Birmingham. One of the local mosques is situated directly opposite the church. The current vicar of St Christopher's, the Revd Toby Howarth, spent several years working in India and the Netherlands, and is the diocesan adviser on interfaith relations. The parish is among the 20 per cent most deprived areas of the city.

As far back as the 1980s, some mums from the church had a vision of a 'stay and play' group for parents and toddlers from the local community, as a 'seedling' that God wanted them to plant. After a hesitant start and a few setbacks, the group began to flourish, initially in people's homes and then later in the church hall. The success of the toddler group led these women and others from the congregation to think about further ways in which the church could engage with its local community. The church members carried out research for a community profile, and a church-based community project, The Springfield Project, was born in 2000, under the banner 'God's love in our community'. It included the stay and play group, a family support team and a nursery.

In 2003, Birmingham City Council approached the church to see if they would be open to a partnership with the council to provide a Sure Start Children's Centre. It would mean knocking down the old church hall and building an entirely new centre—which would cost a cool £2 million. This was clearly a huge decision for the church. In particular, the question in the mind of the congregation was what this partnership would mean for their distinctive identity and witness as a charismatic evangelical church. Would they be able to sustain a distinctively Christian ethos for their project?

St Christopher's discussed the proposal with the relief and mission agency Tearfund, which had long experience of community development both in the UK and overseas. The church also spent time in prayer and fasting and had long discussions among themselves about the proposal. Eventually they decided that it was right to go ahead. Members of the church had also begun to build friendships with the leadership from the mosque and other community leaders, who offered significant and sometimes costly support for the project. The Archbishop of Canterbury was chief guest at the opening ceremony in 2008, which was a great celebration of thanksgiving and praise.

The Springfield Project has now grown to the point where it is becoming too big for the Centre. The original toddler group, Seedlings, now meets three times a week in the main body of the church. Each summer, Seedlings hosts a party for several hundred children and their families from the community. The afternoon features crafts, games and bouncy castles, as well as storytelling from the Bible and activities in which children and their parents or carers can write prayers and bring their concerns to God if they wish to.

The vision of a 'seedling' that God gave a group of mums all those years ago has grown under his hand from a tiny beginning in a front room, until it is now a beautiful 'tree' in which many find shelter, support and love.

8

Fragments and clues

Indiana Jones's bag

By convention, the last part of a book on church leadership should pull together any loose ends and offer clear conclusions, along with specific points for action. However, by definition, that is the one thing you should not find at the end of a book on shaping a unique and creative church. There is no blueprint for how to create a blueprint-free church.

The whole point has been that we each set out on a journey of exploration with a group of fellow travellers, not knowing where that journey will lead us. In a sense, this whole book has simply been an attempt to reassure church leaders who feel uneasy with guardianship models of ministry that they are not alone, and that words such as 'uncertainty', 'improvisation' and 'adventure' have a valid place in church leadership. It has been an attempt to suggest that there is no road, because we make our road as we walk.

But anybody who has seen a classic film of exploration and discovery knows that the adventurer does not head off into the unknown empty-handed. An explorer such as Indiana Jones always carries crucial artefacts in his dusty bag—fragments of ancient maps and shards of old pottery etched with clues that will guide him towards his destination. We may not be able to offer a detailed Ordnance Survey map for the rest of the journey. What we can offer are a few fragments and clues to point fellow explorers in the right direction and help them identify treasure when they find it. The fragments and clues in this chapter pick up on a few of the themes, explicit or implicit, throughout this book so far.

Don't believe the hype

Books on church leadership do not tend to mention the gift of discernment: they tend to focus more on vision, team-building or arguments about apostolic succession. Biblically, on the other hand, discernment appears to be high on the list of God's priorities when it comes to leadership attributes. God appears in a dream to Solomon at the start of his reign in Israel and asks which gift he would most like to receive. Solomon confesses that he feels utterly inadequate to the task of leadership ahead of him, but he asks, 'Give your servant a discerning heart to govern your people and distinguish between right and wrong. For who is able to govern this great people of yours?' (1 Kings 3:9). God is pleased that Solomon has admitted his personal inadequacy and that he has asked not for more self-aggrandising gifts such as long life, wealth or the destruction of his enemies, but for wisdom and discernment, so God grants him his request.

Discernment is the ability to make sound judgments. It involves a capacity to step aside from a situation and point out either what others are unable to see or what they refuse to see. A good model for discernment might be the small boy in *The Emperor's New Clothes* by Hans Christian Andersen, who spots that the emperor has been duped into believing he is wearing fine but invisible clothes. The small boy speaks out and reveals the gullibility of the emperor and the pride of the other onlookers.

Scepticism has a bad reputation among Christians, who conflate it with cynicism or atheism. One dictionary definition of a sceptic is a person who doubts the truth of Christianity and all expressions of religious faith. But our word 'sceptical' comes from the Greek *skepsis*, which actually means an enquiry, examination or reflection (an 'omphalosceptic' is somebody who contemplates their own navel, rather than somebody who doubts that they have one). There is a godly scepticism which is a vital part of discernment because it is prepared to examine both received wisdom and fashionable hype. Biblically, part of wisdom is recognising folly.

Be a pilgrim in your own parish

In my 1999 book *Restoring the Wonder*, I introduced the idea of being a pilgrim in one's own parish. The aim was to help readers to see the familiar with new eyes and appreciate its unique features. By way of example, I referred to my own upbringing in the Warwickshire town of Kenilworth. I apologise for quoting myself at some length, but it does make the point:

Adventure begins on our own doorstep. But few of us realise that, since few of us look at our doorstep. We dream of exotic travel, we fantasise of owning a new home in a chic district, because most of us still believe, deep down, that our level of wonder depends on our environment and our circumstances. But it doesn't... Wonder is a way of seeing. It is our own capacity for engaging passionately with our environment and circumstances, whatever they are. Wonder is not a place we travel to. It is something we carry with us.

Take Kenilworth Castle. What kind of person might look at the majestic ruins of the castle with a maximum sense of wonder? Not the local teenager. His familiarity has dulled his capacity to see it afresh. What about a casual sightseer, on a whistle-stop tour of central England? He would see it, all right. But he would see just another historical curiosity, sandwiched between the grander (and less ruined) Warwick Castle in the morning, and Stratford-on-Avon that evening.

But now meet Jane. She is a student of British history, who lives in

Portland, Oregon. Her specialist subject is Elizabethan England. She has read all about the Earl of Leicester's gardens at Kenilworth: how one of the castle walls was the backdrop to a raised grassy terrace, 10 feet high and 12 feet wide, bearing exquisite white stone ornaments on posts: heraldic beasts, obelisks, balls. Jane has read about the moat which once surrounded Kenilworth Castle, and the feasting and bear-baiting which accompanied the first Queen Elizabeth's visit. She has had her imagination fired by reading Scott's novel.

For years she has dreamed of visiting the places she has read about. So when she can afford the flight to England, her destination is Kenilworth. She travels with the eagerness and passion of a pilgrim: going halfway round the world to see what to somebody else is a small town and a heap of ruins. When she finally enters the castle grounds, she treads with the tread of a pilgrim who knows herself to be walking on holy ground. She looks not with the dulled eyes of the local teenager, or the speedy and superficial eye of the sightseer, but the intense gaze of the pilgrim, for whom every ancient stone becomes an object of amazement.

To encounter a place afresh, I must see it through the eyes of a passionate outsider. To see my own neighbourhood afresh, it must become a place of pilgrimage. I need to become a pilgrim in my own parish.[1]

At the time, I was not writing about church leadership, but the same principle applies to my ministry in a very literal sense. I need to cultivate a capacity to see my own parish as a place of wonder, a place where God is to be found at work in unique and remarkable ways.

Reclaim the wells

When early Christianity reached the county of Derbyshire, it encountered an ancient local tradition of worshipping water spirits in wells and rivers, and holding ceremonies of 'well-dressing' to honour these spirits. Rather than demolishing the wells and denouncing the old customs as idolatrous, the missionaries chose instead to Christianise the ceremonies. The well-dressings were given a new Christian focus of gratitude to God for his gift of water, and many wells were renamed after Christian saints or heroes. A well dedicated to a water sprite called Eilan, for example, was rededicated to St Helen.[2]

Throughout the history of the Church, those engaged in mission to their own culture have had a choice when confronted with native beliefs and practices at odds with Christianity. Should their instinct be to reject or to reclaim them? The Puritan instinct (the default option for most evangelicals, Pentecostals and charismatics) is towards rejection, based on a fear of spiritual contamination and syncretism. The Puritan instinct favours wholesale replacement of the old ways with a 'pure' Christian alternative.

On the other hand, the Celtic instinct, favoured by the early Celtic missionaries of the British Isles and Ireland, was to reclaim the existing traditions. Churches were built on the sites of pagan holy places, standing stones and temples, and beside sacred trees. Events in the old calendar were taken over as feast days of the Christian faith. The Germanic festival of Yule became Christmas, and the Celtic new year festival of Samhain became All Saints.

For Christians immersed in a Puritan mindset, evidence of historical links to paganism entails a betrayal of the true faith. One popular book, *Pagan Christianity?*, aims to expose the 'unscriptural' roots of almost all the familiar elements of the institutional church, including our historic buildings (modelled on Roman basilicas), vestments (based on the dress of Roman officials), patterns of ordained ministry and orders of worship. The authors also condemn church practices that evolved at any stage in Christian history, rather than having an explicit basis in the New Testament. Even an old evangelical staple such as the altar call is denounced because it was introduced by the Methodists rather than having specific biblical sanction. With an enthusiastic leap of logic the authors claim:

If the church is following the life of God who indwells it, it will never produce those nonscriptural practices this book addresses. Such practices are foreign elements that God's people picked up from their pagan neighbours as far back as the fourth century. They were embraced, baptized and called 'Christian'. And that is why the church is in the state it is in today, hampered by endless divisions, power struggles, passivity and lack of transformation among God's people. [3]

The Puritan instinct is suspicious of the local and traditional, which it sees as an expression of humanity in rebellion against the Creator. The Celtic instinct, on the other hand, is to engage the local and traditional, and to use them to point to a faith that helps people make sense of their existing instincts and experiences. The Puritan approach emphasises discontinuity, while the Celtic emphasises continuity. I am convinced that we need to recapture more of the Celtic vision in our day, to engage with our neighbours' existing lifestyles, aspirations and experiences, rather than being shocked by them and dismissing them.

A key biblical model for the Celtic approach to mission is Paul's speech at the Areopagus in Athens (Acts 17:16–34). As others have pointed out, this is a hugely important passage in terms of mission, because it models what an authentic Christian encounter with pagan culture looks like. [4]

The Areopagus was a hill near the Acropolis in Athens, which gave its name to the council that met there. Paul was brought to the Areopagus by a group of Epicurean and Stoic philosophers who wanted to hear more about his beliefs, particularly about the resurrection. At no point in his speech there does Paul quote the Hebrew scriptures. Rather, he structures his address along the lines of a talk by a Stoic philosopher (starting with evidences that the gods exist, followed by pointers to their nature, then demonstrating that the world is ruled by them and that they care for humanity). He opens with a rhetorical device borrowed from Greek authors such as Aristotle and Demosthenes (noting that the people of

Athens are highly religious). Then he refers to an inscription he has spotted during his stay in their own city, 'TO AN UNKNOWN GOD', and uses this as his central image. Even Paul's reference to God not living in temples made by human hands is a quotation from popular authors of the day Zeno, Euripides and Seneca.

Point by point, the rest of Paul's address engages with themes and phrases familiar from Greek philosophy and culture, including the commendation of words from 'some of your own poets', including Epimenides (v. 28). The whole talk enters the world of Greek thought and culture, establishing common ground with Paul's hearers. In this way, Paul uses their own language and logic to point to crucial elements neglected by their philosophy: repentance, judgment and resurrection. It was the moment of conversion for several members of the Areopagus council, including a man called Dionysius.

There is no sense from Paul that it is inappropriate for a Christian to study and enjoy the philosophy, drama and poetry of pagan culture. Quite the opposite: he was clearly immersed in them. Paul's talk at the Areopagus, says screenwriter and Christian author Brian Godawa, 'illustrates a redemptive interaction with those thought forms, a certain amount of involvement in and affirmation of the prevailing culture, in service to the gospel'.[5]

There will unquestionably be times when we have to take a stand against aspects of the surrounding culture, because the gospel judges that which is corrupt in human cultures as well as affirming what is good in them. The early Celtic missionaries sometimes took such a stand, but that did not deter them from their conviction that their primary task was to befriend local cultures, speak their language and reclaim their wells.

Admire and do otherwise

In 1888, the English poet Gerard Manley Hopkins wrote a letter to another poet, Robert Bridges, in which he outlined his philosophy of creativity: 'The effect of studying masterpieces is to make me admire and do otherwise.'

There is much to admire in the best of traditional and contemporary worship done with excellence and 'by the book'. There is much to admire in the life and witness of the great heroes of faith, from the saints, missionaries and teachers of the early church to those of today. There is much to admire in courses and conferences that have been put together with professionalism and after much thought and prayer. There is much to admire in the ministries of gifted church strategists, evangelists and preachers. There may be times when we should go and do likewise, when somebody else's blueprint will be the best solution for our own setting, too. But these times should be rare. Usually, the best course of action will be to admire and do otherwise, to use other people's practice as inspiration for something authentic and home-made.

Bishop Stephen Cottrell, co-author of the popular Emmaus course, recalls a survey conducted to find out which process evangelism course was the most effective: Emmaus, Alpha, or another. The survey found that all the published courses had more or less the same level of effectiveness, with one exception. This one course was significantly more effective when judged in terms of how many people joined a local church afterwards:

It was a home-made course from a parish that was included in the survey as an afterthought. And where can you buy it? Well, you can't. The whole point of the home-made course is that it is home-made. Bucking the trend, confounding the expectations of all those who think that bigger is better and that answers can be found on the shelf, this course was written and produced by those who were going to run it... People had put themselves into it.[6]

The best resources build local flexibility into their model, rather than expecting strict adherence to centrally dictated norms. BRF's Messy Church, for example, is less a franchise to buy into than a broad framework to encourage local creativity with whatever is to hand. It offers a pattern of monthly, weekday events where families can come together to do craft activities, eat, play fun games and worship God.[7]

Christian leaders should not buy into the Romantic myth of the lone genius bursting with natural creativity, while the rest of us lack creativity. Every single one of us can cultivate originality and creativity in our everyday lives, with practices as mundane as remembering to take a pen wherever we go to note down ideas as they occur to us.[8] You are more creative than you think.

Stay away from the mountain

The image of Moses at the top of the mountain is a compelling one. Mount Sinai is surrounded by smoke, the ground shakes, and the whole of the mountain is declared to be so holy that the ordinary people may not approach it on pain of death. There Moses receives God's commandments on behalf of the people (Exodus 19—20). If Moses is our model for Christian leadership, the implication is clear: the leader is the mediator. He ascends the mountain on behalf of the people; he hears a clear word from God, he shares what he has heard, and the life of the people is aligned around it. Classic management theory is not so different: a visionary CEO from an office at the top of the building produces a compelling vision on behalf of the company, whose members then need to be trained and motivated to implement the vision. In both cases, the leader is the chosen one who climbs the mountain while the people wait passively below. To members of declining churches, this model of a strong, charismatic leader with a vision can appear to be the solution to all their problems.

But what if the presence of God is to be found not in the earthquake or the fire, but in a still, small voice? What if his presence is to be found in low-key ways among the people of God, and at work in our local community? What if ordinary people, individually and together, really are the temple where God's Spirit lives? What if the era of the Spirit really is one where ordinary people dream dreams and see visions? In that case, we should not expect our church leaders to be heroic, entrepreneurial CEOs who confidently lead the way and have a clear route in mind. Rather, we should expect them to be listeners, people who create safe spaces for conversations about what God is doing in the everyday and mundane, people who release the imagination and creativity in others.

We should expect our leaders to be people who ask the right questions, rather than knowing the right answers.

Final Snapshot:
Brownswood Park, December 1999

Earlier this week, I went into the church to hear the Highbury Chamber Choir practising for this evening's carol service. I was particularly struck by one of their pieces, and said so to Nicky, their musical director. He replied, 'Yes—it was harmonised by Gibbons.' I'm afraid I stared at him blankly, my lowbrow mind conjuring up images of singing monkeys from *The Jungle Book*. It turned out he meant Orlando Gibbons, the 17th-century English composer. Tonight they were brilliant at the carol service, and the place was packed. The choir even seem to have forgotten that incident in a rehearsal a couple of weeks back, when they were chased around the church by a wild-eyed man with an axe, and had to escape into the vicarage back garden.

At the end of the service, a group of Antiguan old ladies shook my hand and said, 'Thank you, Speedy Vicar', with a wink. They've been calling me that ever since I arranged a family funeral in double-quick time. 'Speedy Vicar': there are worse nicknames I could think of.

It's hard to believe how far we have come since that day when I stood on the doorstep of an unfinished vicarage, wondering what on earth I was going to do to boost an almost non-existent congregation. Most Sundays now, we have about 70 in church. Not massive by some people's standards, but stunning for Brownswood Park. In percentage terms, that's an increase of… what? 700 per cent! We've come to love and value this area, for all its quirks, dysfunctions and oddities. The cheap restaurants from such a massive range of cultures have become a particular highlight, and our children like grabbing a snack from the Happening Bagel Bakery after school. I have to confess, it still irritates me every time I see the word 'bagel' spelt in three different ways on the one shop sign.

Church members keep arriving, finding faith and community, and then disappearing to go off around the world. Sara went to Vancouver, Rosie and Patrick went to set up their business selling African crafts in the Algarve, and Mats and Corinne went back to Sweden. Other people's relatives have been heading back to Montserrat now that the volcano seems to have died down. It's a transient sort of area, so you just get used to the idea that lots of our folk don't stay around for long.

A few weeks back, the Pentecostal college that hires our church hall had a visiting speaker from the States, whom I recognised. He came up to me with a big smile on his face and said just about the last thing I was expecting him to say. He thanked me for introducing his congregation to incense in worship. Apparently, the last time he was over here he had picked up some of my leaflets called 'Things we do in worship, and why'—and he particularly liked the one on incense. He must have found it convincing, because there is now a small Pentecostal church somewhere in the Bible belt that swings an incense thurible during Sunday worship. God has a sense of humour. (Note to self: have a word with our servers, Halil and Sevda, about their habit of using the incense burner to singe my glove puppets when they think I'm not looking. They'll deny it's them, but at least they'll realise I know what they're up to.)

I guess it's true what they say: most church leaders overestimate what they can do in one year, but underestimate what they can do in three or four years. OK, so it's not the most beautiful place in the world, and we're not the biggest or best-resourced church in London. But, for all its limitations, frustrations and eccentric characters, it's our church. And God seems to be doing something unique here.

A prayer for the journey

Lord God,
*   you have called your servants*
*   to ventures of which we cannot see the ending,*
*   by paths as yet untrodden,*
*   through perils unknown.*
Give us faith to go out with good courage,
*   not knowing where we go,*
*   but only that your hand is leading us*
*   and your love supporting us.*
Through Jesus Christ our Lord.
Amen

FROM EVENING PRAYER, *LUTHERAN BOOK OF WORSHIP*

For further reading

Alan Roxburgh, *The Missional Leader* (with Fred Romanuk) (Jossey-Bass, 2006); *Missional Map-Making* (Jossey-Bass, 2010); *Introducing the Missional Church* (with M. Scott Boren) (Baker, 2009).

A paradigm shift in understanding of church and ministry from a Canadian church consultant and former pastor. Roxburgh urges incarnational mission to our local communities and sees the minister primarily as cultivator of the congregation's own wisdom.

Richard Impey, *How to Develop Your Local Church* (SPCK, 2010).

A similar focus to Roxburgh on drawing out the God-given wisdom of the congregation, but in a UK parish context.

Leonard Sweet, *Aquachurch* (Group Publishing, 1999); revised as *Aquachurch 2* (David C. Cook, 2008).

A pioneering vision of a different kind of church leadership for changing times.

Gary Thomas, *Sacred Pathways* (Zondervan, 2000).

Praying as I can, not as I can't. Discovering a model of spirituality that matches my temperament.

Erik Rees, *S.H.A.P.E.* (Zondervan, 2006).

A Christian guide to discovering our unique gifts and calling.

Paul Kingsnorth, *Real England: The Battle Against the Bland* (Portobello Books, 2008).

A rousing protest against the destruction of local and regional differences and the rise of clone towns. Uses England as an example, but similar principles apply elsewhere.

Twyla Tharp, *The Creative Habit* (Simon & Schuster, 2003).

A practical guide to making creativity part of your everyday life, by a leading New York choreographer. Not written with church leaders in mind, but many of her principles apply.

Notes

Chapter 1: A very personal journey

1 Mike Starkey, *Fashion & Style* (Monarch, 1995).
2 Mike Starkey, *Restoring the Wonder* (SPCK/Triangle, 1999).
3 G.K. Chesterton, *The Outline of Sanity* (Methuen, 1926).
4 Leonard Sweet, *Aquachurch* (Group Publishing, 1999); *Summoned to Lead* (Zondervan, 2004); Erwin Raphael McManus, *An Unstoppable Force* (Group Publishing, 2001).
5 Including John Drane, *Faith in a Changing Culture* (HarperCollins, 1997); John Drane, *Cultural Change and Biblical Faith* (Paternoster, 2000); John Drane, *Do Christians Know How to be Spiritual?* (DLT, 2005); Brian McLaren, *The Church on the Other Side* (Zondervan, 2000); Brian McLaren, *Finding Our Way Again* (Thomas Nelson, 2008); see also J. Richard Middleton and Brian Walsh, *Truth is Stranger Than it Used to Be* (SPCK, 1995).
6 Stuart Murray, *Post-Christendom* (Paternoster, 2004); *Church After Christendom* (Paternoster, 2005).
7 For a good overview, see Eddie Gibbs and Ryan Bolger, *Emerging Churches* (SPCK, 2006).
8 *Mission-Shaped Church* (CHP, 2004).
9 Alan J. Roxburgh and M. Scott Boren, *Introducing the Missional Church* (Baker, 2009); Alan J. Roxburgh, *Missional Map-Making* (Jossey-Bass, 2010); Alan J. Roxburgh and Fred Romanuk, *The Missional Leader* (Jossey-Bass, 2006).
10 Vincent Donovan, *Christianity Rediscovered* (SCM, 1978/1982).
11 Donovan, *Christianity Rediscovered*, p. 16.
12 Donovan, *Christianity Rediscovered*, p. 2.
13 Ed Young, *The Creative Leader* (Broadman & Holman, 2006), p. 125.

Chapter 2: Cloning the church

1 A. Simms, *Tescopoly* (Constable, 2007), p. 24.
2 Sociologist George Ritzer calls this process the McDonaldization of society. See Ritzer, *The McDonaldization of Society* (Pine Forge Press, 1993).

3 Andrew Simms, Julian Oram, Alex MacGillivray, Joe Drury, *Ghost Town Britain* (New Economics Foundation, 2002), p. 23.
4 London Assembly report, 'Cornered Shops' (July 2010).
5 Paul Kingsnorth, *Real England* (Portobello Books, 2008), p. 152.
6 A few authors have applied the McDonaldization thesis to the church. See John Drane, *The McDonaldization of the Church* (DLT, 2000), and *After McDonaldization* (DLT, 2008); Eddie Gibbs and Ryan Bolger, *Emerging Churches* (SPCK, 2006), pp. 174–175. Sociologist Stephen Hunt applies it specifically to the rise of the Alpha course. See Stephen Hunt, 'Packing them in the aisles?' in Louise Nelstrop and Martyn Percy (eds), *Evaluating Fresh Expressions* (Canterbury Press, 2008).
7 Lynne and Bill Hybels, *Rediscovering Church* (Zondervan, 1997).
8 For a creative alternative to church cloning, see Stuart Murray, *Planting Churches* (Paternoster, 2008).

Chapter 3: The call to creativity

1 Sweet, *Aquachurch*, p. 93.
2 Paul C. Vitz, *Psychology as Religion: the Cult of Self-Worship*, second edition (Eerdmans, 1994), Chapter 2.
3 David F. Wells, *No Place for Truth* (Eerdmans, 1993), p. 185.
4 Paul D. Tieger and Barbara Barron, *Do What You Are*, revised edn (Little, Brown, 2007). On page 190 we are told the INTJ personality combination is one that yearns to 'create and develop original and innovative solutions'. The list of possible jobs includes scientific researcher, anthropologist, writer, architect and critic; no jobs in spiritual or pastoral leadership are suggested. On the other hand, the ESFJ personality (p. 268) aspires to establishing 'warm and genuine interpersonal relationship with other people, working in real and tangible ways to improve their quality of life'. Suggested jobs for this type include religious educator and minister/priest/rabbi.
5 Sweet, *Aquachurch*.
6 Josh McDowell, *Evidence that Demands a Verdict* (Here's Life Publishers, 1972, plus revised editions).
7 Robert Banks, *God the Worker* (Albatross, 1992); Starkey, *Fashion & Style*.
8 Richard J. Mouw, *When the Kings Come Marching In: Isaiah and the New Jerusalem* (Eerdmans, 2002).
9 Brian Godawa, *Word Pictures* (IVP, 2009), p. 136.

10 At a popular level, see Steve Turner, *Imagine: a Vision for Christians in the Arts* (IVP, 2001); Michael Card, *Scribbling in the Sand: Christ and Creativity* (IVP, 2002). At a more scholarly level, see Jeremy Begbie, *Voicing Creation's Praise: Towards a Theology of the Arts* (T&T Clark, 1991).

11 Erwin Raphael McManus, *An Unstoppable Force* (Group Publishing, 2001), p. 48.

12 James Bell, Jill Hopkinson and Trevor Willmott (eds), *Re-Shaping Rural Ministry* (Canterbury Press, 2009), p. 6.

13 Ian Birrell, 'There has never been a better time to be alive', *London Evening Standard* (4 January 2011), p. 14.

14 Paul Collier, *The Bottom Billion* (Oxford University Press, 2008).

15 Will Hutton, *The Observer* (4 April 2010), p. 23.

16 James A. Herrick, *The Making of the New Spirituality* (IVP, 2003); Drane, *Do Christians Know How to be Spiritual?*; John Drane, *What is the New Age Still Saying to the Church?* (HarperCollins, 1999).

17 John Micklethwait and Adrian Wooldridge, *God is Back* (Allen Lane, 2009).

18 Martyn Percy, *Clergy: the Origin of Species* (Continuum, 2006), p. 163.

19 Roxburgh and Romanuk, *The Missional Leader*, p. 6.

20 A.M. Allchin, *God's Presence Makes the World* (DLT, 1997), p. 125.

Chapter 4: Unique church

1 Bill Hybels, *Courageous Leadership* (Zondervan, 2002), pp. 123, 129.

2 *Mission-Shaped Church*, p. 104.

3 Martyn Percy, 'A vision for initial ministerial education', in Bell, Hopkinson and Willmott (eds), *Re-Shaping Rural Ministry*, p. 146.

4 There are professionals who carry out audits on behalf of churches. Manchester Diocese has a helpful brief guide to mission audits at www.manchester.anglican.org/church-society/doing-a-parish-audit (accessed 26/10/2010). This sort of survey can be done in a more informal way by the leader and church members together. Other resources include Tearfund's excellent *Discovery* course, which aims to equip local churches to respond to needs in their own community, and the training on understanding a local community offered by the Street Pastors initiative.

5 Drane, *Do Christians Know How to be Spiritual?* p. 17.

6 *Mission-Shaped Church*, p. 4.
7 Eugene Peterson, *The Wisdom of Each Other* (Zondervan, 1998), p. 55.
8 Richard Impey, *How to Develop Your Local Church: Working With the Wisdom of the Congregation* (SPCK, 2010), p. 8.
9 John Drane, *Faith in a Changing Culture* (HarperCollins, 1997), ch. 8.
10 A helpful resource is Sue Pickering, *Spiritual Direction* (Canterbury Press, 2008).
11 Lesslie Newbigin, *The Gospel in a Pluralist Society* (SPCK, 1989); see particularly ch. 8.
12 Newbigin, *Gospel in a Pluralist Society*, ch. 5.
13 Newbigin, *Gospel in a Pluralist Society*, p. 18.
14 Murray, *Post-Christendom*.
15 Allan Hirsch, *The Forgotten Ways* (Brazos Press, 2007).
16 McManus, *Unstoppable Force*, p. 31.

Chapter 5: Unique leader

1 Erik Rees, *S.H.A.P.E.: Finding and Fulfilling Your Unique Purpose for Life* (Zondervan, 2006), ch. 5.
2 Bill Hybels, *Holy Discontent* (Zondervan, 2007).
3 Michael Mangis, *Signature Sins* (IVP, 2008).

Chapter 6: Rethinking vision

1 Hybels, *Courageous Leadership*, p. 48.
2 John Maxwell, *The 21 Indispensable Qualities of a Leader* (Thomas Nelson, 1999), p. 150.
3 See Ian Stackhouse, *The Gospel-Driven Church* (Paternoster, 2004), ch. 1.
4 Jo Owen, *The Death of Modern Management* (Wiley, 2009); Roxburgh, *Missional Map-Making*.
5 Will Mancini, *Church Unique* (Jossey-Bass, 2008), p. 25.
6 Jim Collins, *Good to Great* (Random House, 2001).
7 Owen, *Death of Modern Management*, p. 53.
8 John Kay, *Obliquity* (Profile Books, 2010), p. 44.
9 Kay, *Obliquity*, p. 46.
10 Roxburgh, *Missional Map-Making*, p. 76.
11 Amiel Osmaston, 'Leadership models and skills', in Bell, Hopkinson and Willmott (eds), *Re-Shaping Rural Ministry*, p. 58.
12 R.T. France, *Divine Government* (SPCK, 1990).

13 One of the 'Seven Marks of a Healthy Church' identified by Springboard, the Church of England Archbishops' Initiative for Evangelism.

14 Roxburgh and Boren, *Introducing the Missional Church*, ch. 11.

15 Roxburgh and Boren, *Introducing the Missional Church*, p. 152.

16 Roxburgh and Boren, *Introducing the Missional Church*, p. 165.

17 Impey, *How to Develop Your Local Church*.

Chapter 7: Rethinking guidance

1 For a theological model of the idea that God takes risks, see Clark Pinnock et al., *The Openness of God* (IVP, 1994); John Sanders, *The God Who Risks*, second edition (IVP, 2007).

2 For example, Garry Friesen, *Decision Making and the Will of God* (Multnomah, 1980); Ron Kinkaid, *Praying for Guidance* (IVP, 1996); Haddon Robinson, *Decision-Making by the Book* (Victor Books, 1991). This chapter draws particularly on Friesen.

3 Charles F. Stanley, *God Has a Plan for Your Life* (Thomas Nelson, 2008), p. 11.

4 Stanley, *God Has a Plan for Your Life*, p.13.

5 Brad Long, Paul Stokes and Cindy Strickler, *Growing the Church in the Power of the Holy Spirit* (Zondervan, 2010).

6 Long, Stokes and Strickler, *Growing the Church*, p. 14.

7 Long, Stokes and Strickler, *Growing the Church*, p. 41.

8 Long, Stokes and Strickler, *Growing the Church*, p. 25.

9 Haddon Robinson, foreword to Friesen, *Decision Making and the Will of God*, p. 13; See also Robinson, *Decision-Making by the Book*, pp. 15–19.

10 Leland Ryken, *Worldly Saints: the Puritans as They Really Were* (Zondervan, 1986), ch. 2. See also R. Paul Stevens, 'Vocational guidance', in *The Complete Book of Everyday Christianity* (IVP, 1997), p. 1078.

11 Friesen, *Decision Making and the Will of God*, ch. 19.

12 Quotation from talks by Cardinal Suenens at Fountain Trust conferences in the UK during the 1970s.

Chapter 8: Fragments and clues

1 Starkey, *Restoring the Wonder*.

2 Michael Mitton, *Restoring the Woven Cord* (BRF, 2010), p. 96.

3 Frank Viola and George Barna, *Pagan Christianity?* (Tyndale/Barna Books, 2008), p. xx.

4 See commentaries on Acts. Also Godawa, *Word Pictures*, ch. 6; Drane, *Do Christians Know How to be Spiritual?*, pp. 111f.; Stephen Rost, 'Paul's Areopagus speech in Acts 17', in Irving Hexham, Stephen Rost and John W. Morehead II (eds), *Encountering New Religious Movements* (Kregel, 2004).

5 Godawa, *Word Pictures*, p. 135.

6 Stephen Cottrell, *Hit the Ground Kneeling* (CHP, 2008), p. 60.

7 Lucy Moore, *Messy Church* (BRF, 2006); *Messy Church 2* (BRF, 2009).

8 Twyla Tharp, *The Creative Habit* (Simon & Schuster, 2003).

Also from BRF

Pioneers 4 Life

Explorations in theology and wisdom
for pioneering leaders

Edited by David Male

There is a growing awareness that the Church must commit to radically new agendas and fresh initiatives in order to connect the gospel with the widest possible spectrum in our society. Faith, commitment, sacrifice and boldness are needed—and an emerging generation of pioneering leaders focused on breaking new ground and growing Christian communities where none has flourished for many years, if ever.

This multi-contributor book emerges from the strategic thinking and shared experiences of those attending the Breakout Pioneers Conference (www.breakoutpioneer.org.uk), an annual three-day gathering of pioneer church leaders, both lay and ordained, from across the denominations. Established to seek out and draw together pioneers, the gathering also looks to support and train them so that they are free to pioneer as God leads them.

Contributors include Richard Bauckham, Graham Cray, John Drane, Lucy Moore and Mark Russell.

ISBN 978 1 84101 827 0   £8.99
*Available from your local Christian bookshop
or from www.brfonline.org.uk.*

Also from BRF

The Challenge of Change

A guide to shaping change and changing
the shape of church

Phil Potter

Change can feel uncomfortable and risky, but these days it is an ever-increasing force in society and will continue to have a dominating effect on how we view our world. Decisions on what and how and when we change will inevitably affect growth or decline in a church and also have a major impact on people. Leaders can end up burnt out by their attempts to bring about change or by facing up to the challenge of it, while congregations are left damaged and disillusioned because they could not catch the vision.

This book offers a map for healthy and godly change. Writing as a pastor and practitioner, Phil Potter explains ways of shaping all kinds of change in the life of a church, particularly in the context of the fresh expressions emerging. This is a book that speaks to reluctant traditionalists and impatient visionaries, to both struggling and thriving congregations. Also included are over 100 questions for personal and group reflection.

ISBN 978 1 84101 604 7   £7.99
Available from your local Christian bookshop
or from www.brfonline.org.uk.

About
brf:

BRF is a registered charity and also a limited company, and has been in existence since 1922. Through all that we do—producing resources, providing training, working face-to-face with adults and children, and via the web— we work to resource individuals and church communities in their Christian discipleship through the Bible, prayer and worship.

Our Barnabas children's team works with primary schools and churches to help children under 11, and the adults who work with them, to explore Christianity creatively and to bring the Bible alive.

To find out more about BRF and its core activities and ministries, visit:

www.brf.org.uk
www.brfonline.org.uk
www.biblereadingnotes.org.uk
www.barnabasinschools.org.uk
www.barnabasinchurches.org.uk
www.faithinhomes.org.uk
www.messychurch.org.uk
www.foundations21.org.uk

If you have any questions about BRF and our work, please email us at

enquiries@brf.org.uk

enter